DISCARD

crochet edgings & trims

THE HARMONY GUIDES

crochet
edgings
& trims

150 stitches

edited by Kate Haxell

INTERWEAVE
interweavestore.com

First published in the United States by
Interweave Press LLC
201 East Fourth Street
Loveland, CO 80537-5655
Interweavestore.com

ISBN: 978-1-59668-172-9

Technical Editor: Luise Roberts

Picture credits:
front cover, 14 Holly Jolliffe
2, 8, 10, 18 Michael Wicks
Istock 6 above left, below right
All stitch diagrams by Karen Manthey
All other photography by Geoff Dann

10 9 8 7 6 5 4 3 2 1

Reproduction by Dot Gradations Ltd, UK
Printed and bound by 1010 Printing International Ltd, China

contents

inspiration

This carefully selected collection of designs will prove an invaluable resource for any crocheter, whether they are looking for classic patterns or contemporary ideas.

This new Harmony Guide of 150 crochet edgings and trims will inspire the novice and experienced crocheter alike with ribs, laces, appliqués, fringes, ruffles, and borders. Whatever your tastes and skills, there will be patterns here that will have you reaching for your hook and yarn.

Appreciation of the unique is not a new phenomenon: traditionally, beautiful linens for the home were embellished with fine crochet and so the craft came to represent the formality of the very best. These household items that were so lovingly created display a wealth of ingenuity and expertise that many a modern volume draws upon. A delicate place mat pattern worked in a sport-weight yarn becomes a shawl. The last few rounds of the same place mat become an edging.

Crochet is popular as a trimming for several reasons: it is quick to do, hard wearing, and infinitely flexible to work. After all, there is only one stitch to concentrate on at any given time, and the next stitch can take a variety of forms and positions. A single stitch also makes it easier to use almost any fiber, from wool and cotton to leather and wire, because the individual loops and gauge are easy to adjust from one stitch to the next.

Crochet is the perfect way to personalize a project with a design detail that will make a simple idea stand out and be noticed. A small pattern can be made bold with a change of fiber. An edging can be made crisp and sculptural or delicate and light by changing the gauge and the hook size.

Create a lacy border for a cuff, a rose to adorn a hat, or a pillow with crisp trim appliquéd in stripes. Improve the drape of an afghan blanket with a narrow beaded edge, lengthen a much-loved child's garment with a fresh, decorative hem detail, or update a favorite accessory with one of the many patterns in this book.

The speed at which crochet can be worked makes it a quick way to experiment with a variety of swatches and to create long lengths of trim. Explore, learn, and enrich your crochet appreciation by simply working some of the swatches in this book. You will be surprised what you find and new project ideas will flow as freely as the fiber you choose to work with.

tools & equipment

It is sometimes hard to believe that beautiful and intricate-looking crochet is created using only two essential tools—a crochet hook and the yarn itself.

Crochet Hooks

Crochet hooks are usually made from steel, aluminium, or plastic in a range of sizes according to their diameter. As each crochet stitch is worked separately until only one loop remains on the hook, space is not needed to hold stitches.

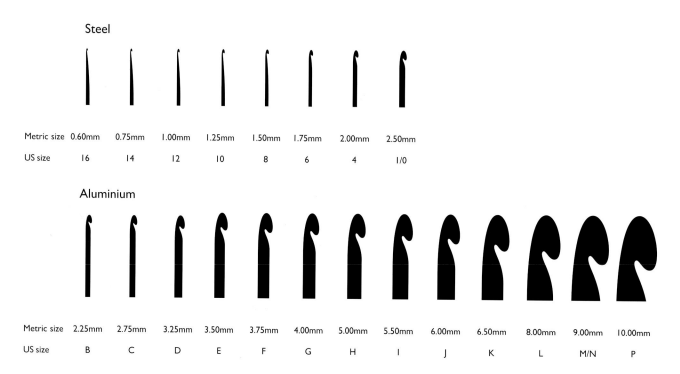

Steel

Metric size	0.60mm	0.75mm	1.00mm	1.25mm	1.50mm	1.75mm	2.00mm	2.50mm
US size	16	14	12	10	8	6	4	1/0

Aluminium

Metric size	2.25mm	2.75mm	3.25mm	3.50mm	3.75mm	4.00mm	5.00mm	5.50mm	6.00mm	6.50mm	8.00mm	9.00mm	10.00mm
US size	B	C	D	E	F	G	H	I	J	K	L	M/N	P

Crochet Yarns

Traditionally, crochet was worked almost exclusively in very fine cotton yarn to create or embellish household items such as table cloths, doilies, cuffs, and frills. The samples in this book were worked in a wool/cotton yarn, but may take on a totally different appearance if different yarns are used. Lacier stitches probably look their best in smooth threads, but some of the all-over stitches can be more interesting when worked in tweedy or textured yarns. Crochet yarns can now be found in leather, suede, and even fine jewellery wire.

Holding the Hook and Yarn

There are no hard and fast rules as to the best way to hold the hook and yarn. The diagrams below show one method, but choose whichever way you find the most comfortable.

Due to the restrictions of space it is not possible to show diagrams for both right- and left-handed people. Left-handers may find it easier to trace the diagrams and then turn the tracing paper over, thus reversing the image; alternatively, reflect the diagrams in the mirror. Read left for right and right for left where applicable.

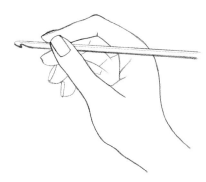

The hook is held in the right hand as if holding a pencil.

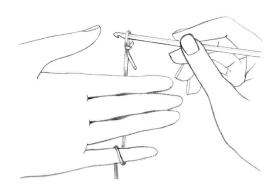

To maintain the slight tension in the yarn necessary for easy, even working, it can help to arrange the yarn around the fingers of the left hand in this way.

The left hand holds the work and at the same time controls the yarn supply. The left hand middle finger is used to manipulate the yarn, while the index finger and thumb hold on to the work.

Note: Right-handers work from right to left and left-handers from left to right.

the basics

The patterns in this book use the following basic stitches. They are shown worked into a foundation chain, but the method is the same whatever part of the work the stitch is worked into.

Slip Knot

Almost all crochet begins with a slip knot. Make a loop, then hook another loop through it. Tighten gently and slide the knot up to the hook.

Yarn Over (yo)

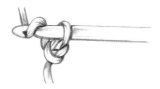

Wrap the yarn from back to front over the hook (or hold the yarn still and maneuver the hook). This movement of the yarn over the hook is used over and over again in crochet, and is usually abbreviated as "yo."

Chain Stitch (ch)

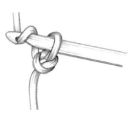

1 Yarn over and draw the yarn through to form a new loop without tightening up the previous one.

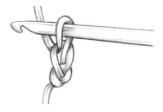

2 Repeat to form as many chains as required. Do not count the slip knot as a stitch. **Note:** Unless otherwise stated, when working into the foundation chain always work under two strands of chain loops, as shown in the following diagrams.

Slip Stitch (sl st)

This is the shortest of crochet stitches and, unlike other stitches, is not used on its own to produce a fabric. It is used for joining, shaping, and, where necessary, carrying the yarn to another part of the fabric for the next stage.

1 Insert the hook into the work (second chain from hook in diagram), yarn over and draw the yarn through both the work and loop on the hook in one movement.

2 To join a chain ring with a slip stitch, insert the hook into first chain, yarn over and draw the yarn through the work and the yarn on the hook.

Single Crochet (sc)

1 Insert the hook into the work (second chain from hook on foundation chain), *yarn over and draw the yarn through the work only.

2 Yarn over again and draw the yarn through both loops on the hook.

3 1sc made. Insert hook into next stitch; repeat from * in step 1.

Half Double Crochet (hdc)

1 Yarn over and insert the hook into the work (third chain from hook on foundation chain). *Yarn over and draw through the work only.

2 Yarn over again and draw through all three loops on the hook. 1hdc made. Yarn over, insert hook into next stitch; repeat from * in step 1.

Double Crochet (dc)

1 Yarn over and insert the hook into the work (fourth chain from hook on foundation chain). *Yarn over and draw through the work only. Yarn over and draw through the first two loops only.

2 Yarn over and draw through the last two loops on the hook. 1dc made. Yarn over, insert hook into next stitch; repeat from * in step 1.

Triple Crochet (tr)

1 Yarn over twice, insert the hook into the work (fifth chain from hook on foundation chain). *Yarn over and draw through the work only.

2 Yarn over again and then draw through the first two loops only.

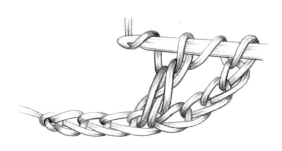

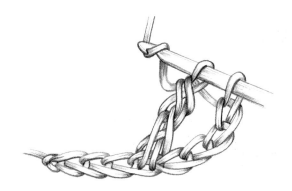

3 Yarn over again and then draw through the next two loops only.

4 Yarn over again and draw through the last two loops on the hook.

Longer Basic Stitches

Double treble (dtr), triple treble (ttr) and quadruple treble (quadtr) are made by wrapping the yarn over three to five times at the beginning and finishing as for a triple, repeating step 3 until two loops remain on hook, finishing with step 4.

making fabric

These are the basic procedures for making crochet edgings—the things that crochet patterns sometimes assume you know. These principles can be applied to all the patterns in this book.

Foundation Chain

An edging can be worked from a foundation chain or from the edge of a fabric. The length of the foundation chain is the number of stitches needed for the first row of fabric, plus the number of chains needed to get to the correct height of the stitches to be used in the first row. If working along the edge of a fabric, join in the yarn and work the number of skipped chains specified at the beginning of the first row.

Working in Rows

For the first row either count and work into the chains or, if working along a fabric, the equivalent distance along the edge of the fabric. At the beginning of each row one or more chains must be worked to bring the hook up to the desired height—the number depends upon the height of the stitch to be used:

    single crochet = 1 chain

    half double crochet = 2 chains

    double crochet = 3 chains

    triple = 4 chains

    When working half double crochet, or longer stitches, the turning chain takes the place of the first stitch. Where one

chain is worked at the beginning of a row foundation with single crochet, it is usually for height only and is in addition to the first stitch, so it is not included in the stitch count.

Basic Double Fabric

Make a foundation chain of the required length plus two chains. Work one double crochet into fourth chain from hook. The three chains at the beginning of the row form the first double crochet. Work one double crochet into the next and every chain to the end of the row.

At the end of each row, turn the work so that another row can be worked across the top of the previous one. It does not matter which way the work is turned, but be consistent.

Make three chains for turning. These turning chains will count as the first double crochet. and so skip the first double crochet in the previous row. Work a double crochet into the top of the next and every double crochet including the last double crochet in row, then work a double crochet into the third of three chains at the beginning of the previous row.

Placement of Stitches

All crochet stitches (except chains) require the hook to be inserted into existing work. It has already been shown how to work into a chain and into the top of a stitch, but stitches can also be worked into the following places.

Working into Chain Spaces

When a stitch, group, shell, cluster, or bobble is positioned over a chain or chains, the hook is often inserted into the space under the chain.

It is important to note whether the pattern instructions stipulate working into a particular chain as this will change the appearance of the design. This information may be given as a note.

A stitch group that is worked into a chain space as shown, spreads out over more than one stitch; therefore on the stitch diagrams they will not be closed at the base.

Working Around the Stem of a Stitch

Inserting the hook around the whole stem of a stitch creates raised or relief effects.

Working around the front of the stem gives a stitch that lies on the front of the work.

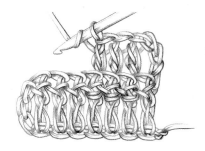

Working around the back of the stem gives a stitch that lies on the back of the work.

Working In the Front or Back Loop Only

Inserting the hook under one loop at the top of the stitch leaves the other loop as a horizontal bar.

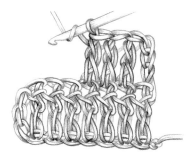

In front loop.

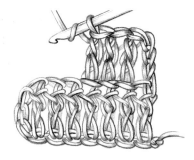

In back loop.

Working rows or rounds of front or back loops

If you work rows consistently into the front loop only, you will make a series of ridges alternately on the back and front of the work. Working rows into the back loop only makes the ridges appear alternately on the front and back of the work. Working rounds always into the front loop only will form a bar on the back of the work, and vice versa.

If, however, you work alternately into the front loop only on one row and then the back loop only on the next row, the horizontal bars will all appear on the same side of the fabric.

Working Between Stitches

Inserting the hook between the stems of the stitches produces an open effect.

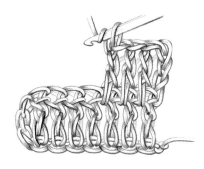

Ensure that the number of stitches remains constant as it is easy to miss the first or last space.

Increasing and Decreasing

In the case of edgings, the rapid increase or decrease of the number of stitches is a common method of creating a ruffle or frill. Increasing is generally achieved by working two or more stitches in the pattern where there would normally be one stitch. Conversely, decreasing is achieved by working two or more stitches together, or skipping one or more stitches. However, stitches are often grouped in crochet and on following rows it is important to recognize accurately the position of the stitches. Groups of stitches shown on a stitch diagram may be, for example, bobbles, and not necessarily mean that the fabric will flare or make a ruffle.

Joining in New Yarn and Changing Color

When joining a new yarn or changing color, work in the old yarn until two loops of the last stitch remain.

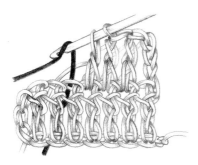

Use the new color or yarn to complete the stitch. Work the following stitches in the new color or yarn.

Joining yarn to an edge

When joining a new length of yarn to an edge of a textile or knitted or crocheted fabric, insert the hook into the nearest strong point to the edge, wrap the yarn over the hook and draw it through the fabric. Then, work one chain with the tail end and continue working as the pattern suggests.

Gauge

Edgings are generally worked at a tighter gauge than crochet fabric. This gives it an extra durability and crispness. However, it is important to consider the gauge of the fabric being edged and if the fabric is a crochet fabric created from a pattern instruction, then the pattern will prove to be an invaluable guide to the gauge of the edging.

The gauge is usually specified as a number of stitches and a number of rows to a given measurement (usually 4 in/10cm). The quick way to check is to make a square of fabric about 6 in (15cm) wide in the correct pattern and with the correct yarn and suggested hook size, lay this down on a flat surface and measure it—first horizontally (for stitch gauge) and then vertically (for row gauge). If your square has too few stitches or rows to the measurement, your gauge is too loose and you should try again with a smaller hook. If it has too many stitches, try a larger hook. Stitch gauge is generally more important than row gauge in crochet.

If the project has no gauge instruction, then work a series of swatches of your chosen edging or edgings, varying the hook size and the perhaps the fiber until one edging makes the design statement you require. Use this swatch to calculate your gauge.

Once the gauge is established, use it to calculate the number of repeats along an edge and, if working directly into an edge, to plan the stitch placement on the first row.

Fastening Off

To fasten off the yarn permanently, break off the yarn about 2 in (5cm) away from the work (longer if you need to sew pieces together). Draw the end through the loop on the hook and tighten gently.

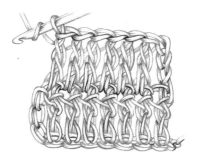

stitch variations

Different effects can be created by small variations in the stitch-making procedure or by varying the position and manner of inserting the hook into the fabric.

Filet Crochet

This is a particular technique of crochet based on forming designs from a series of solid and open squares called "blocks" and "spaces." These are more often used in crochet lace patterns made with cotton, but can be worked in knitting yarn.

Shells

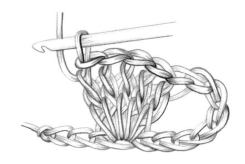

These consist of several complete stitches worked into the same place. They can be worked as part of a pattern or as a method of increasing.

On stitch diagrams, the point at the base of the group will be positioned above the space or stitch where the hook is to be inserted.

Clusters

Any combination of stitches may be joined into a cluster by leaving the last loop of each temporarily on the hook until they are worked off together at the end. Working stitches together in this way can also be a method of decreasing.

It is important to be sure exactly how and where the hook is to be inserted for each "leg" of the cluster. The "legs" may be worked over adjacent stitches, or stitches may be skipped between "legs."

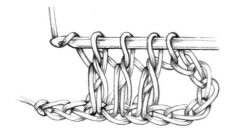

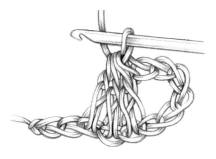

1 Work stitches into each of the positions indicated in the pattern, leaving the last loop of each stitch on the hook.

2 Yarn over and draw through all the loops on the hook. On diagrams, each "leg" of the cluster will be positioned above the stitch where the hook is to be inserted.

Bobbles

When a cluster is worked into one stitch, it forms a bobble.

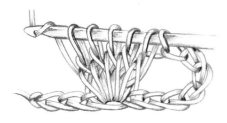

1 Work the stitches indicated by the pattern into one position, leaving the last loop of each on the hook.

2 Yarn over and draw through all the loops on the hook. Bulky bobbles can be secured with an extra chain stitch—if this is necessary, it will be indicated within the pattern.

Popcorns

Popcorns are groups of complete stitches usually worked into the same place, folded and closed at the top. An extra chain can be worked to secure the popcorn. They're great for adding textural interest to a garment.

1 Work the stitches indicated by the pattern into one position. Take the hook out of the working loop and insert it into the top of the first stitch (here, double crochet) made, from front to back.

2 Pick up the working loop and draw this through to close the popcorn. If required, work one chain to secure the popcorn. On stitch diagrams, the point at the base of the popcorn will be positioned above the space or stitch where it is to be worked.

Puff Stitches

These are similar to bobbles but worked using half double crochet. As half double crochet cannot be worked until one loop remains on the hook, the stitches are not closed until the required number have been worked.

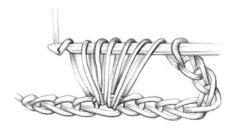

1 Yarnover, insert the hook, yarn over again and draw a loop through (three loops on the hook). Repeat this step as specified, inserting the hook into the same stitch; yarn over and draw through all the loops on the hook.

2 An extra chain stitch is often used to secure the puff stitch firmly. This will be indicated within the pattern if necessary. A **cluster** of half double crochet stitches is worked in the same way as a puff stitch but each "leg" is worked where indicated.

Picots

A picot is normally a chain loop formed into a closed ring by a slip stitch or single crochet.

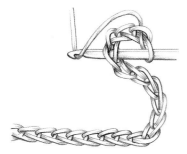

1 Work four chains. Into the fourth chain from the hook, work a slip stitch to close. Continue working chains or required stitch.

Crossed Stitches

This method produces stitches that are not entangled with each other and so maintain a clear "X" shape.

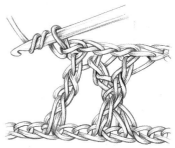

1 Skip two stitches and work the first stitch into next stitch. Work one chain, then work the second stitch into the first of the skipped stitches, taking the hook behind the first double before inserting. See individual pattern instructions for variations on crossed stitches.

stitch
gallery

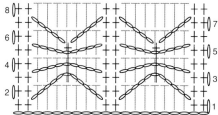

Grouped Relief Strands

Multiple of 9 sts + 2 sts (add 1 st for base chain).

1st row (right side): 1sc into 2nd ch from hook, *1sc in next ch, 11ch, skip 7 ch, 1sc into next ch; rep from * to last ch, 1sc into last ch, turn.

2nd row: 1ch, 1sc into first st, *1sc into next sc, working in front of 11ch-sp, 1hdc into each of 7 skipped ch of 1st row, 1sc into next sc; rep from * to last st, 1sc into last ch, turn.

3rd row: 1ch, 1sc into first st, *1sc into next sc, 9ch, skip 7 hdc, 1sc into next sc; rep from * to last st, 1sc into last ch, turn.

4th row: 1ch, 1sc into first st, *1sc into next sc, working in front of 9ch-sp, 1dc into each of 7 skipped hdc of 2nd row, 1sc into next sc in 3rd row; rep from * to last st, 1sc into last ch, turn.

Rep 3rd and 4th rows.

7th row: 1ch, 1sc into first st, *1sc into next sc, 5ch, insert hook under 3 chain strands of previous rows and work 1sc around the 3 chain strands, 5ch, 1sc into next sc; rep from * to last st, 1sc into last ch, turn.

Rep 2nd row.

Fasten off.

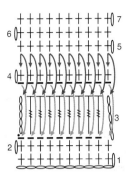

Long-stitch Pintucks

Worked lengthways over any number of sts (add 1 st for base chain).

1st row (right side): 1sc into 2nd ch from hook, 1sc into each ch to end, turn.

2nd row: 1ch, 1sc into each sc to end, turn.

3rd row: 5ch (count as 1 dtr) 1dtr into front loop of each sc to last sc, 5ch, sl st into last st, turn.

4th row: 1ch, 1sc into unworked top loop (now front loop) of each sc of 2nd row, turn.

5th row: 1ch, *insert hook through next sc and corresponding dtr or tch from 3rd row, yo, draw loop through the layers, yo, to complete a sc st; rep from * to end, turn.

6th row: 1ch, 1sc into each sc to end, turn.

7th row: 1ch, 1sc into each sc to end, turn.

Rep 3rd to 7th rows until required length is reached. Fasten off.

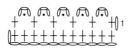

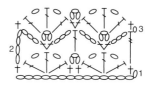

Picot Edging

Multiple of 2 sts + 1 st (add 1 st for base chain).

Special abbreviation: picot = 3ch, sl st into 3rd ch from hook.

Note: work foundation row if working from a base chain.

Foundation row: 1sc into 2nd ch from hook and each ch to end, turn.

1st row (right side): 1ch, 1sc into first st, *picot, skip 1 st, 1sc into next st; rep from * to end.

Fasten off.

Open Shell with Picot

Multiple of 7 sts (add 1 st for base chain).

Special abbreviations: shell = (1dc, 1ch, 1dc, 1ch, 1dc) in ch or sp indicated; **picot** = (1sc, 3ch, 1sc) in st indicated.

1st row (right side): 1sc into 2nd ch from hook, *skip 2 ch, work a shell into next ch, skip 2 ch, 1sc into next ch**, 3ch, 1sc into next ch; rep from * ending last rep at **, turn.

2nd row: 7ch (count as 1tr and 3 ch), *skip 1 dc and 1 ch, work a picot into next dc of shell, 3ch**, 1dc into next 3ch-arch, 3ch; rep from * ending last rep at **, 1tr into last sc, skip tch, turn.

3rd row: 1ch, 1sc into first st, *skip next 3ch-sp, shell into next picot**, skip next 3ch-sp, picot into next dc; rep from * ending last rep at **, 1sc into 4th ch of tch.

Fasten off.

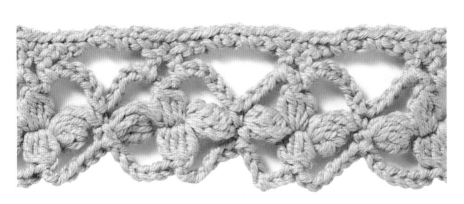
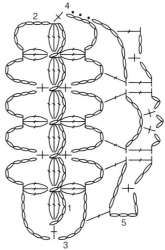

Floral Diamonds

Worked lengthways.

Special abbreviation: bobble = work 3dc into next ch or st indicated leaving 1 loop of each on hook, yo and draw through all 4 loops on hook.

1st row (right side): *5ch, 1 bobble into 5th ch from hook; rep from * until required length is reached with an even number of bobbles, do not turn but rotate work 90 degrees and proceed to work along one long edge.

2nd row: 7ch, 1 bobble into base of first bobble, *7ch, 1sc into base of next bobble **, 7ch, 1 bobble into base of next bobble; rep from * ending last rep at **, do not turn but rotate work 180 degrees and proceed to work along the other long edge.

3rd row: Rep 2nd row, ending with last sc in top of last bobble, turn at end of row.

4th row: Sl st into each of next 3 ch, 7ch (count as 1 dc, 4 ch), *1dc in each of next 2 ch-sps **, 7ch; rep from * ending last rep at **, 4ch, 1dc into 4th ch of tch, turn.

5th row: *5ch (count as 1 dc, 2 ch), 1sc in 4ch-sp, 2ch, 1dc in each of next 2 dc, [2ch, 1sc in ch-sp] twice, 2ch, 1dc in each of next 2 dc; rep from * to last dc, 2ch, 1sc in ch-sp, 2ch, 1dc in 3rd ch of tch.

Fasten off.

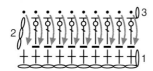

Beaded Pintuck

Multiple of any number of sts (add 1 st for base chain).

Special abbreviation: beaded-dc = yo, insert hook into next st, yo, draw loop through, yo, draw yarn through 2 loops, slide bead along yarn to base of hook, yo, draw yarn through remaining 2 loops.

Note: thread beads onto yarn before starting.

1st row (right side): 1sc into 2nd ch from hook, work 1sc into each ch to end, turn.

2nd row: 3ch (count as 1 dc) skip st at base of ch, * 1 beaded-dc into front loop of each sc to end, turn.

3rd row: 1ch, *insert hook through next dc and corresponding back loop from the st on 2nd row, yo, draw loop through the layers to complete a sl st; rep from * to end.

Fasten off.

Cluster Arch Edging

Multiple of 4 sts + 1 st (add 1 st for base chain).

Special abbreviation: dc2tog = 1dc into next st leaving 1 loop of st, skip 1 st, 1dc into next leaving 1 loop of st on hook, yo and through all 3 loops on hook.

Note: work foundation row if working from a base chain.

Foundation row: Using A, 1sc into 2nd ch from hook and each ch to end, turn.

1st row (right side): 1ch, 1sc into first st, *3ch, dc2tog, 3ch, 1sc into next st; rep from * to end.
Fasten off. Do not turn.
Join in B into first sc st.

2nd row: 1ch, 1sc into first sc, *3ch, skip 3 ch, 1sc into next dc2tog, 3ch, skip 3 ch, 1sc into next sc; rep from * to end.
Fasten off.

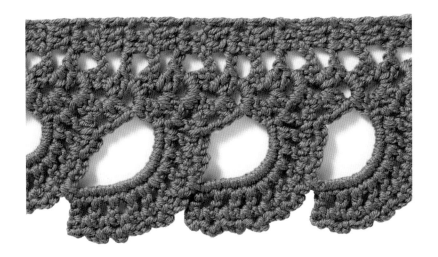

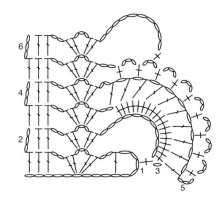

Quarter-roundel Edge

Worked lengthways.

1st row (right side): 15ch, 1dc into 6th ch from hook, 2ch, skip 3 ch, (2dc, 3ch, 2dc) into next ch, 2ch, skip 2ch, 1dc into into each of next 3 ch, turn.

2nd row: 3ch (count as 1dc), skip st at base of ch, 1dc into each of next 2 dc, 2ch, skip 2ch-sp and next 2 dc, (2dc, 3ch, 2dc) into next 3ch-sp, 10ch, skip 2ch-sp and next dc, 1sc into 6ch-sp, turn.

3rd row: 1ch, 18sc into 10ch-sp, 2ch, skip 2 dc, (2dc, 3ch, 2dc) into next 3ch-sp, 2ch, skip 2 dc and 2ch-sp, 1dc in each of next 2 dc, 1dc into top of tch, turn.

4th row: 3ch, (count as 1 dc), skip st at base of ch, 1dc into each of next 2 dc, 2ch, skip 2ch-sp and next 2 dc, (2dc, 3ch, 2dc) into next 3ch-sp, 2ch, skip 2 dc, 1dc into next 2ch-sp, [1ch, skip next sc, 1dc into next sc] 9 times, turn.

5th row: [3ch, 1sc in next 1ch-sp] 9 times, 2ch, skip 1dc, 2ch-sp and 2 dc, (2dc, 3ch, 2dc) into next 3ch-sp, 2ch, 1dc in each of next 2 dc, 1dc into top of tch, turn.

6th row: 3ch (count as 1dc), skip st at base of ch, 1dc into each of next 2 dc, 2ch, skip 2ch-sp and next 2 dc, (2dc, 3ch, 2dc) into next 3ch-sp, 10ch, skip next 2 dc, 2ch-sp and next 3ch-sp, 1sc into 3ch-sp, turn.

Rep 3rd to 6th rows until required length is reached, ending with a 5th row.

Fasten off.

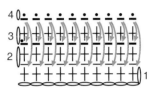

Slip Stitch Edge

Multiple of any number of sts (add 1 st for base chain).

Note: this edging is worked onto a background fabric of double crochet stitches.

1st row (right side): 1sc into 2nd ch from hook, 1sc into each ch or equivalent interval to end, turn.

2nd row: 1ch, 1sc into back loops of each sc to end. Fasten off. Do not turn.

Return to start of 2nd row. Join yarn under front loop of first sc.

3rd row: 1ch, 1sc into front loops of each sc to end. Fasten off. Do not turn.

Return to start of row. Join contrasting yarn into inside top loop of first st of 2nd row, 1ch.

Rotate the work 90 degrees, so the 2 rows of sc st are parallel and facing away from you. Position yarn so it is lying between the 2 rows of sc.

4th row: *Insert hook from top to bottom through inside top loop of sc from first row, insert hook from top to bottom through inside top loop of sc from 2nd row, yo, complete a sl st; rep from * to end.

Fasten off.

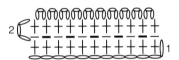

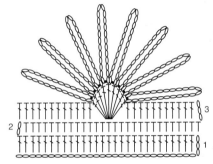

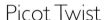

Picot Twist

Multiple of 2 sts + 1 st (add 1 st for base chain).

1st row (right side): 1sc into 2nd ch from hook and each ch to end, turn.

2nd row: 3ch, 1sc into back loop of first st, *3ch, 1sc into front loop of next st, 3ch, 1sc into back loop of next st; rep from * to end.

Fasten off.

Dandelion Dangle

Multiple of 17 sts + 12 sts (add 2 sts for base chain).

1st row (right side): Skip 3 ch (count as 1 dc) and 1dc into next ch, work 1dc into each ch to end, turn.

2nd row: 2ch, work 1hdc into each st to end, turn.

3rd row: 3ch (count as 1 dc), skip st at base of ch, work 1dc in each of next 11 sts, *skip next 2 hdc, work into next hdc ([1dc, 24ch, sl st into back of first ch] 8 times, 1dc), skip 2 hdc, 1dc in each of next 12 sts; rep from * to end.

Fasten off.

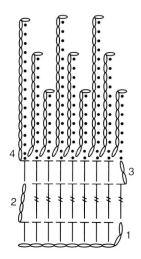

Undulating Fringe

Multiple of 3 sts (add 1 st for base chain).

1st row (wrong side): Skip 2 ch (count as 1 hdc), 1 hdc into next ch, 1 hdc into each ch to end, turn.

2nd row: 4ch (count as 1 tr), 1 tr into each st to end, turn.

3rd row: 2ch (count as 1 hdc), 1 hdc into each st to end, turn.

4th row: *16ch, sl st into back bump of 2nd ch from hook, 1 sl st into back bump of each ch, 1 sl st into next hdc, 12ch, sl st into back bump of 2nd ch from hook, 1 sl st into back bump of each ch, 1 sl st into next hdc, 8ch, sl st into back bump of 2nd ch from hook, 1 sl st into back bump of each ch, 1 sl st into next hdc; rep from * to end. Fasten off.

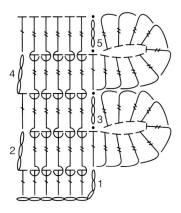

Loop Ruffle

Worked lengthways over 7 sts (add 2 sts for base chain).

Special abbreviations: tr/rf (raised triple crochet at the front of the fabric) = yo twice, insert hook from in front and from right to left around the stem of the appropriate stitch, and complete stitch normally; **tr/rb** (raised triple crochet at the back of the fabric) = yo twice, insert hook from behind and from right to left around the stem of the appropriate stitch, and complete stitch normally.

1st row: Skip 3 ch (count as 1 dc) and 1dc into next ch, 1dc into each ch to end, turn.

2nd row: 3ch, [tr/rf around next st, tr/rb around next st] twice, tr/rf around next st, 1dc into top of tch, *yo twice, insert hook from front to back around post of last st, yo, and complete a tr st; rep from * 8 more times, turn.

3rd row: Skip first 9 tr, sl st into top of last dc forming ring of tr, 3ch, sl st into base of last tr of ring, [tr/rf around next st, tr/rb around next st] twice, tr/rb around next st, 1dc onto top of tch, turn.

Rep 2nd and 3rd rows until required length is reached, ending with a 2nd row.

Fasten off.

Cartwheel Fringe

Multiple of 13 sts + 7 sts (1 motif for each repeat).

Special abbreviations: tr/rf (raised triple crochet at the front of the fabric) = yo twice, insert hook from in front and from right to left around the stem of the appropriate stitch, and complete stitch normally; **tr/rb** (raised triple crochet at the back of the fabric) = yo twice, insert hook from behind and from right to left around the stem of the appropriate stitch, and complete stitch normally.

Motif

Base ring: 4ch, join with sl st to form ring.

1st round: Work 8sc into ring, sl st to first sc.

2nd round: 5ch (count as 1hdc and 3ch), skip sc at base of 5ch, hdc into next sc, *3ch, hdc into next sc; rep from * 5 more times, 3ch, sl st to 2nd ch of tch. Each hdc forms a spoke.

3rd round: 1ch, 1sc into first st, *4sc into next 3ch-sp, 1sc into next hdc; rep from * around, omitting last sc. sl st to first sc.
Fasten off.

Header

Foundation chain: 7ch *tr/rb around a hdc of a motif, 4ch, tr/rb around next spoke of same motif, 7ch; rep from * to end, turn.

1st row: 3ch, skip 3 ch (count as 1dc) and 1dc into next ch, 1dc into each of next 5 ch, *tr/rb around post of next st, 1dc in each of next 4 ch, tr/rb around post of next st, 1dc into each of next of next 7 ch; rep from * to end, turn.

2nd row: 3ch (count as 1dc) skip dc at base of ch, 1dc into each of next 6 dc, *tr/rf around post of next st, 1dc in each of next 4 dc, tr/rf around post of next st, 1dc into each of next of next 7 dc; rep from * to end.
Fasten off.

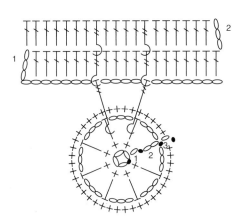

Jekyll Border

Multiple of 24 sts + 1 st (add 4 sts for base chain).

Special abbreviations: dc2tog = work 2dc into next st leaving 1 loop of each on hook, yo and through all 3 loops on hook; **bobble** = work 4dc into next st leaving 1 loop of each on hook, you and through all 5 loops on hook; **group** = work 1dc into next st, then into same st as last dc work [1ch, 1dc] twice.

1st row (right side): Skip 4 ch (count as 1dc, 1 ch) and 1dc into next ch, skip 2 ch, 1sc into next ch, skip 2 ch, 1 group into next ch, skip 2 ch, 1sc into next ch, skip 2 ch, 5dc into next ch, *skip 2 ch, 1sc into next ch, [skip 2 ch, 1 group into next ch, skip 2 ch, 1 sc into next ch] 3 times, skip 2 ch, 5dc into next ch; rep from * to last 12 ch, skip 2 ch, 1sc into next ch, skip 2 ch, 1 group into next ch, skip 2 ch, 1sc into next ch, skip 2 ch, into last ch work (1dc, 1ch, 1dc), turn.

2nd row: 1ch, 1sc into first dc, 1 group into next sc, 1sc into center dc of next group, skip 1 dc, 2dc into each of next 5 dc, *1sc into center dc of next group, [1 group into next sc, 1sc into center dc of next group] twice, skip 1 dc, 2dc into each of next 5 dc; rep from * to last group, 1sc into center dc of next group, 1 group into next sc, skip (1dc, 1 ch), 1sc into next ch, turn.

3rd row: 4ch (count as 1dc, 1 ch), 1dc into first sc, 1sc into center dc of first group, 2ch, skip next (1ch, 1dc, 1sc), [1 bobble between next pair of dc, 2ch] 5 times, *1sc into center dc of next group, 1 group into next sc, 1sc into center dc of next group, 2ch, [1 bobble between next pair of dc, 2ch] 5 times; rep from * to last group, 1sc into center dc of last group, into last sc work, (1dc, 1ch, 1dc), turn.

4th row: 1ch, 1sc into first dc, *4ch, 1dc into next 2ch-sp, [4ch, 1dc into top of next bobble, 4ch, 1dc into next 2ch-sp] 5 times, 4ch, 1sc into center dc of next group; rep from * to end, placing last sc into 3rd ch of tch. Fasten off.

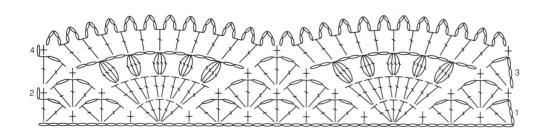

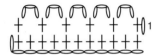

Chain Arch Edging

Multiple of 2 sts + 1 st (add 1 st for base chain).

Note: work foundation row if working from a base chain.

Foundation row: 1sc into 2nd ch from hook and each ch to end, turn.

1st row (right side): 1ch, 1sc into first st, *3ch, skip 1 st, 1sc into next st; rep from * to end.

Fasten off.

Diagonal Spike Edge

Multiple of 4 sts + 2 sts (add 2 sts for base chain).

Special abbreviation: sdc (spike double crochet) = yo, insert hook from front to back round first dc of previous 3dc block worked, yo, draw loop through and up so as not to crush 3dc block, [yo, draw through 2 loops] twice.

1st row: Skip 3 ch (count as 1dc) and 1dc into next ch, *1dc into next ch, 3ch, sl st into 3rd ch from hook, 1dc into next ch, work 1sdc, skip 1 ch, dc into next ch; rep from * to end.

Fasten off.

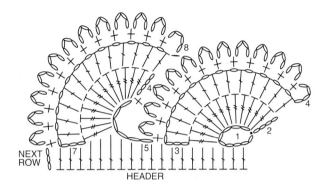

Fan Frills

Worked lengthways.

1st row (right side): 9ch, sl st to join.

2nd row: 4ch (count as 1 tr), 12 tr into ring, turn.

3rd row: 4ch (count as 1 dc, 1 ch), [1dc into sp between 2tr, 1ch] 11 times, 1dc into sp between last tr and tch, turn.

4th row: [4ch, 1sc into next 1ch-sp] 12 times, turn.

5th row: 6ch, skip 4ch-sp, 1sc into next 4ch-sp, turn.

6th row: 4ch (count as 1 tr), 12tr into 6ch-sp, turn.

7th row: 4ch (count as 1 dc, 1ch), [1dc into sp between 2tr, 1ch] 11 times, 1dc into sp between last tr and tch, 1sl st into 5th 4ch-sp of 5th row, turn.

8th row: [4ch, 1sc into 1ch-sp] 12 times, turn.

Rep 5th to 8th rows until required length is reached. Rotate work 90 degrees and work along the edge without scallops.

Header

Next row: 3ch (count as 1dc), 1dc into equivalent st interval to end.

Fasten off.

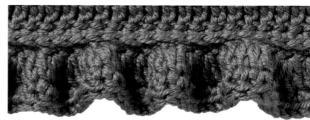

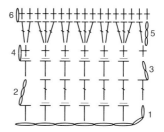

Corded Edging

Multiple of any number of sts (add 1 st for base chain).
Special abbreviation: reverse sc = working from left to right, 1sc into st to the right, keeping the working yarn to the left of hook.

1st row (right side): 1sc into 2nd ch from hook, work 1sc into each ch to end. Do not turn.

2nd row: 1ch, *1 reverse sc into next st to right; rep from * to end.

Fasten off.

Simple Ruffle

Multiple of 2 sts + 1 st (add 1 st for base chain).

1st row (right side): Skip 2 ch, (count as 1 hdc), 1hdc into next ch, 1hdc into each ch to end, turn.

2nd row: 3ch (count as 1 dc), 1dc into back bar under top loops of each hdc to end, turn.

3rd row: 2ch (count as 1 hdc), 1hdc into each dc to end, turn.

4th row: 1ch, 1sc into back bar under top loops of each hdc to end, turn.

5th row: 3ch (count as 1 dc), 1dc into st at base of ch, *3dc into next sc, 2dc into next sc; rep from * to end, turn.

6th row: 1ch, 1sc into each dc to end.

Fasten off.

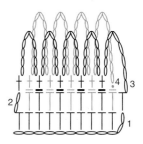

Long Loop Fringe

Multiple of 2 sts + 1 st (add 1 st for base chain).

Using yarn A work a base chain the required length.

1st row (right side): Skip 2 ch (count as 1 hdc), 1hdc into next ch, 1hdc into each ch to end, turn.

Join in yarn B.

2nd row: Using yarn A, 2ch (count as 1 hdc), *using yarn B, yo, insert hook into next st, draw yarn through st, drop yarn B, carry yarn A over yarn B, using yarn A, yo, draw through all loops on hook, using yarn A, yo, insert hook into next st, draw yarn through st, drop yarn A, carry yarn B over yarn A, using yarn B, yo, draw through all loops on hook; rep from * to end, turn.

Fasten off yarn B.

3rd row: Using yarn A, *10ch, 1sc into front loop of next yarn A hdc top loops; rep from * to end, do not turn.

Fasten off yarn A.

Return to start of 3rd row. Rejoin yarn B under back loop of first yarn B hdc top loops.

4th row: Using yarn B, *14ch, 1sc into front loop of next yarn B hdc top loops; rep from * to end.

Fasten off.

Fringe of Strands

Multiple of 4 sts + 1 st (add 1 st for base chain).

Special abbreviation: bobble = work 3dc into next ch or st indicated leaving 1 loop of each on hook, yo and through all 4 loops on hook.

Note: using a piece of thick card slightly deeper than the required fringe, wrap yarn round the card, cutting the yarn along one edge to create strands. For a thicker fringe use more strands in some or all of the strand chains in the 2nd row.

1st row (right side): 1sc into 2nd ch from hook, 1sc into back bump of each ch to end, turn.

2nd row: With WS facing, remove hook from the working loop, *insert hook through next st, place the center of a folded strand over hook, and draw through the loop on the hook, pass the ends through the loop and hang the strands down to the RS; rep from * to end. Do not turn.

3rd row (wrong side): Position hook back through the working loop, 1ch, *1sc into each st inserting hook through same sts that were worked in 2nd row, between the strands looped through each st; rep from * to end, do not turn.

4th row: With WS facing, remove hook from the working loop, *insert hook through next st, place the center of a folded strand over the hook, and draw through the loop on the hook, pass the ends through the loop and hang the strands down to the RS; rep from * to end, turn.

5th row (right side): Place hook back through the working loop, 1ch, *1sc into each st inserting hook through the same sts that were worked in 4th row, between the strands looped through each st; rep from * to end, turn.

6th row (wrong side): 1ch, *insert hook through foundation ch ch-loops and next st, yo, to complete a sc st; rep from * to end, turn.

7th row: 4ch (counts as 1dc, 1 ch), *skip 1 sc, 1 bobble into next sc, 1ch, skip 1 sc, 1dc into next sc **, 1ch; rep from * ending last rep at **, turn.

8th row: 1ch, *1sc in next dc, 1sc in ch-sp, 1sc in bobble, 1sc in ch-sp; rep from * to last ch-sp, 1sc into tch, turn.

9th row: 1ch, 1sc into each sc to end.

Fasten off.

Strip Loops

Multiple of 6 sts + 3 sts (add 1 st for base chain).

1st row (right side): 1sc into 2nd ch from hook, work 1sc into each ch to end, turn.

2nd row: 1ch, 1sc into each sc to end, turn.

3rd row: 1ch, sl st into first st, *[12ch, sl st into 3rd ch from hook, sl st into each of rem ch, sl st into next sc] twice, insert hook through 2ch-sp at end of last tail and into next st, yo, draw loop through all the layers and loop on hook, pass first tail through loop just created, insert hook through 2ch-sp at end of first tail and into next st, yo, draw loop through all the layers and loop on hook**, sl st in each of next 3 sc; rep from * ending last rep at **, sl st into last st.

Fasten off.

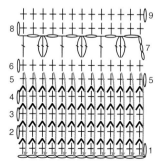

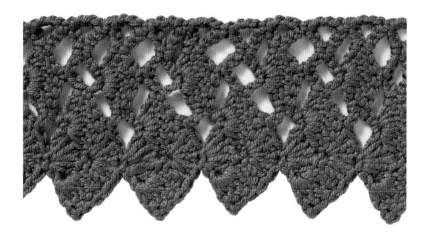

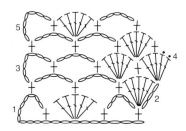

Cluster Diamonds

Worked lengthways.

1st row (wrong side): 20ch, 1sc into 11th ch from hook, skip 2 ch, 5dc into next ch, skip 2ch, 1 sc into next ch, 5ch, skip 2 ch, 1 sc into next ch, turn.

2nd row: 3ch, 5dc into first st, 1sc into next 5ch-sp, 5ch, skip 2 dc, 1sc into next dc, 5ch, skip 2 dc, 1sc into 3rd ch of tch, turn.

3rd row: 7ch, 1sc into next 5ch-sp, 5ch, 1sc into next 5ch-sp, 5dc into next sc, skip 2 dc, 1sc into next dc, skip 2 dc, 5dc into top of tch, turn.

4th row: 1ch, sl st into each of next 2 dc, 1sc into next dc, skip 2 dc, 5dc into next sc, skip 2 dc, 1sc into next dc, 5ch, 1sc into next 5ch-sp, 5ch, 1sc into 3rd ch of tch, turn.

5th row: 7ch, 1sc into next 5ch-sp, 5dc into next sc, 1sc into next 5ch-sp, 5ch, skip 1 sc and 2 dc, 1sc into next dc, turn.

Rep 2nd to 5th rows until required length is reached, ending with a 5th row.

Fasten off.

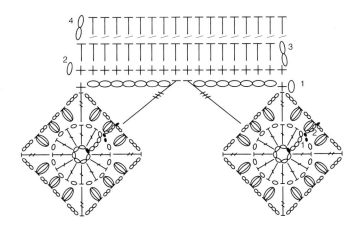

French Square

Multiple of 9 sts (1 motif for each repeat).

Special abbreviation: puff stitch = [yo, insert hook into sp, yo and draw loop through] 4 times, yo and draw through all loops on hook.

Motif

Base ring: 6ch, join with sl st to form ring.

1st round (right side): 4ch (count as 1dc and 1ch), [1dc into ring, 1ch] 11 times, sl st to 3rd of tch. (12 spaces)

2nd round: Sl st into next sp, 3ch, work puff stitch into same sp (counts as puff stitch), *2ch, work puff stitch into next sp, 3ch, 1tr into next dc, 3ch, work puff stitch into next sp, 2ch**, puff stitch into next sp; rep from * twice more and from * to ** again, sl st to top of first puff stitch.

Header

With right side facing, join in yarn through top of tr at corner of square.

1st row: 1ch, 1sc into top of same tr, *7ch, counting along the edge of the motif, skip next 3ch-sp and next 2ch-sp, 1dtr into next 2ch-sp along motif edge, 1dtr into the corresponding 2ch-sp on next motif, 7ch, working along the edge of the motif, 1sc into next tr on corner, counter-clockwise from last dtr; rep from * until all squares have been joined, turn.

2nd row: 1ch, work 1sc into each st to end, turn.

3rd row: 2ch, work 1hdc into each st to end, turn.

4th row: 2ch, work 1hdc into back bar (below top loops) of each st to end.

Fasten off.

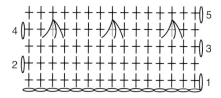

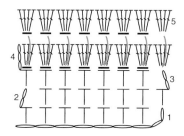

Crow's Foot Edging

Multiple of 5 sts (add I st for base chain).

Special abbreviation: spc (spike cluster) = insert hook through fabric 3 times, first to right, then below, then to left of next st, each time yo, drawing yarn up to height of edging row, insert hook into next st, yo, draw loop through, (5 loops on hook), ending yo, draw through all loops.

Ist row (right side): Isc into 2nd ch from hook, work Isc into each ch to end, turn.

2nd row: Ich, Isc into first st, work Isc into each st to end, turn.

Rep 2nd row twice more.

5th row: Ich, Isc into each of first 2 sts, *Ispc over next st, Isc into next of each 4 sts; rep from* to end, omitting 2sc at end of last rep.

Fasten off.

Close Fan Ruffle

Multiple of any number of sts (add I st for base chain).

Ist row (right side): Skip 2 ch, (count as I hdc), Ihdc into next ch, Ihdc into each ch to end, turn.

2nd row: 2ch (count as I hdc), Ihdc in each st to end, turn.
Rep 2nd row.

4th row: 3ch (counts as I dc), 3dc into base of ch, *4dc into front loop of next hdc; rep from * to end, turn.

5th row: 4dc into unworked top loop (now front loop) of each hdc of 3rd row.

Fasten off.

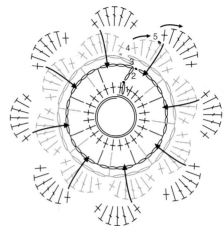

Rose Garden

Note: all the roses shown are worked from the same pattern but the number of rounds worked has been varied. The number of rounds worked for each rose motif is as follows: left, all five rounds; middle, 1st to 4th rounds only; right, 1st to 2nd rounds only.

Motif

Wind the yarn 3 or 4 times around a finger, remove the loop from finger and fasten with a sl st.

1st round: 1ch, 24sc into ring, sl st to first sc.

2nd round: 6ch (count as hdc and 4ch), skip next 2 sc, 1hdc into next sc, [4ch, skip 2 sc, 1hdc into next sc] 6 times, 4ch, sl st to 2nd ch of tch.

3rd round: 4ch, working in sc in 1st round, behind sts in 2nd round, skip 3 sc, 1hdc into next st, *3ch, skip next 2 sc, 1hdc into next sc; rep from * 6 times more, 3ch, sl st into 2nd ch of first tch, turn.

Working back along the two rounds of chains just worked, work foll two rounds:

4th round: (1sc, 1hdc, 3dc, 1hdc, 1sc) into each 3ch-sp from round 3, sl st to first sc.

5th round: Sl st into last 4ch-sp of round 2, (1sc, 1hdc, 3dc, 1hdc, 1sc) into each 4ch-sp from round 2, sl st to first sc. Fasten off.

Slip stitch motifs to fabric.

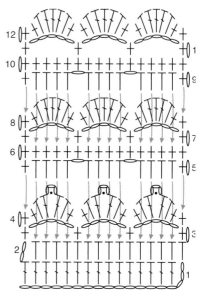

Layered Shells

Multiple of 5 sts + 1 st (add 2 sts for base chain).

1st row: Skip 3 ch (count as 1 dc) and 1dc into next ch, work 1dc into each ch to end, turn.

2nd row: 2ch, 1hdc into each st to end, turn.

3rd row: 1ch, 1sc into first st, 5ch, skip 4 hdc, 1sc into next st; rep from * to end, turn.

4th row: 1ch, 1sc into first st, *(1sc, 1hdc, 1dc, 3ch, sl st into 3rd ch from hook, 1dc, 1hdc, 1sc) into next 5ch-sp; rep from * to last sc, 1sc into next sc, turn.

5th row: 1ch, 1sc into first st, working behind shells in 4th row, 1hdc into next 4 hdc skipped on 3rd row, *1ch, working behind shells in 4th row, 1hdc into next 4 hdc skipped on 3rd row; rep from * to last sc, 1sc into next sc, turn.

6th row: 1ch, 1sc into first st, 1sc into each st and 1ch-sp to end of row, turn.

7th row: 1ch, 1sc into first st, *5ch, skip 4 sc, 1sc into next st; rep from * to end, turn.

8th row: 1ch, 1sc into first st, *(1sc, 1hdc, 3dc, 1hdc, 1sc) into next 5ch-sp; rep from * to last sc, 1sc into next sc, turn.

9th row: 1ch, 1sc into first st, working behind shells in 8th row, 1hdc into next 4 sc skipped on 7th row, *1ch, working behind shells in 8th row, 1hdc into next 4 sc skipped on 7th row; rep from * to last sc, 1sc into next sc, turn.

Rep 6th to 8th rows once more.

Fasten off.

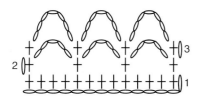

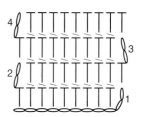

Simple Chain Loops

Multiple of 4 sts + 1 st (add 1 st for base chain).

1st row (right side): 1sc into 2nd ch from hook, work 1sc into each ch to end, turn.
2nd row: 1ch, 1sc into first sc, *5ch, skip 3 sc, 1sc into next sc; rep from * to end, turn.
3rd row: 1ch, 1sc into first sc, *7ch, 1sc into next sc; rep from * to end.
Fasten off.

Faux Knitted Rib

Worked lengthways over any number of sts (add 1 st for base chain).

1st row (right side): Skip 2 ch, (count as 1 hdc) 1hdc into next ch, 1hdc into each ch to end, turn.
2nd row: 2ch, 1hdc into back bar under top loops of each hdc to end, turn.
Rep 2nd row until required length is reached.
Fasten off.

Cable Edge

Worked lengthways over 10 sts, (add 1 st for base chain).

Special abbreviations: tr/rf (raised triple crochet at the front of the fabric) = yo twice, insert hook from in front and from right to left around stem of appropriate stitch, and complete stitch normally; **tr/rb** (raised triple crochet at the back of the fabric) = yo twice, insert hook from behind and from right to left around the stem of the appropriate stitch, and complete stitch normally.

Note: in this pattern, the stitch behind the tr/rb is skipped.

1st row (right side): 1sc into 2nd ch from hook, work 1sc into each ch to end, turn.

2nd row: 2ch (counts as first hdc), hdc in each sc to end, turn.

3rd row: 2ch (counts as first hdc), tr/rf around next st, hdc in next st, tr/rf around each of next 4 sts, hdc in next st, tr/rf around next st, hdc in top of tch, turn.

4th row: 2ch (counts as first hdc), tr/rb around next st, hdc in next st, tr/rb around each of next 4 sts, hdc in next st, tr/rb around next st, hdc in top of tch, turn.

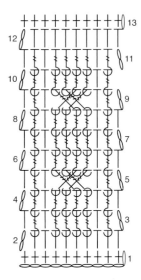

5th row: 2ch (counts as first hdc), tr/rf around next st, hdc in next st, skip next 2 sts, tr/rf around each of next 2 sts; next, working in front of 2 sts just worked, tr/rf around each of 2 skipped sts, hdc in next st, tr/rf around next st, hdc in top of tch, turn.

6th row: 2ch (counts as first hdc), tr/rb around next st, hdc in next st, tr/rb around each of next 4 sts, hdc in next st, tr/rb around next st, hdc in top of tch, turn.

Rep 3rd to 6th rows until required length is reached, ending with a 6th row.

Next row: 2ch (counts as first hdc), hdc in each sc to end, turn.

Next row: 1ch, 1sc into each ch to end, turn.
Fasten off.

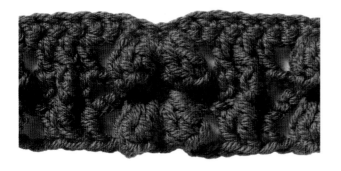

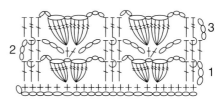

Zigzag Popcorns

Multiple of 10 sts + 3 sts (add 1 st for base chain).

Special abbreviations: 5dc-popcorn = work 5dc into indicated st, remove hook from working loop, insert hook under top loops of first of the dc sts just worked, hook the working loop and draw this through the top loops to draw the popcorn closed, ch1; **tr/rf** (raised triple crochet at the front of the fabric) = yo twice, insert hook from in front and from right to left around the stem of the appropriate stitch, and complete stitch normally; **tr/rb** (raised triple crochet at the back of the fabric) = yo twice, insert hook from behind and from right to left around the stem of the appropriate stitch, and complete stitch normally.

Note: work foundation row if working from a base chain.

Foundation row: 1sc into 2nd ch from hook and each ch to end, turn.

1st row (right side): 3ch (count as 1dc), 1dc into each of next 2 sts, *3ch, skip 3 sts, 5dc-popcorn into next st, 1ch, 5dc-popcorn into next st, 2ch, skip 2 sts, 1dc into each of next 3 sts; rep from * to end, turn.

2nd row: 3ch (count as 1dc), skip first st, 1tr/rb around next st, 1dc into next st, *3ch, skip 1ch-sp and 5dc-popcorn, 2sc into next 1ch-sp, 3ch, skip 5dc-popcorn and 2ch-sp, 1dc into next st, 1tr/rb around next st, 1dc into next st; rep from * ending last rep in top of tch, turn.

3rd row: 3ch (count as 1dc), skip first st, 1tr/rf around next st, 1dc into next st, *3ch, skip 3ch-sp, 5dc-popcorn into next sc, 1ch, 5dc-popcorn into next sc, 2ch, skip 3ch-sp, 1dc into next st, 1tr/rf around next st, 1dc into next st; rep from * ending last rep in top of tch.

Fasten off.

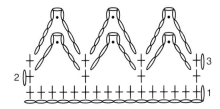

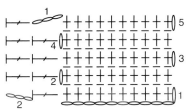

Picot Points

Multiple of 5 sts + 1 st (add 1 st for base chain).

Special abbreviation: 5ch-picot = 5ch, sl st into back bar of 3rd ch from hook; **6ch-picot** = 6ch, sl st into back bar of 3rd ch from hook.

1st row (right side): 1sc into 2nd ch from hook, work 1sc into each ch to end, turn.

2nd row: 1ch, 1sc into first sc, * 5ch-picot, 3ch, skip next 4 sc, 1sc into next sc; rep from * to end, turn.

3rd row: 1ch, 1sc into first sc, *6ch-picot, 4ch, 1sc into next sc; rep from * to end.

Fasten off

Ridged Single Crochet

Worked lengthways over any number of sts (add 1 st for base chain).

1st row (right side): 1sc into 2nd ch from hook, 1sc into each ch to end, turn.

2nd row: 1ch, 1sc into back loop of each sc to end, turn. Rep 2nd row until required length is reached. Do not turn but rotate the work 90 degrees and proceed to work along one long edge.

Header

1st row: 3ch (count as 1 dc), 1dc into edge st at end of each previous row to end, turn.

2nd row: 3ch (count as 1 dc), 1dc into each dc to end. Fasten off.

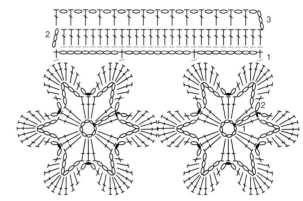

Flower Border

Multiple of 9 sts + 1 st (1 motif for each repeat).

Motif

Base ring: 8ch, join with sl st.

1st round: 3ch (count as 1 dc), 1dc into ring, [6ch, 3dc into ring] 5 times, 6ch, 1dc into ring, sl st to top of tch.

2nd round: *1ch, (1sc, 1hdc, 7dc, 1hdc, 1sc) into next 6ch-sp, 1ch, skip 1 dc, 1 sl st into next dc; rep from * 5 more times placing last sl st into top of tch of previous round.

Fasten off.

Header

With right side facing join yarn to back bar of center dc of motif petal.

1st row: 1ch, 1sc same place as yarn has been joined, 8ch, sc into back bar of center dc of next petal, *9ch, sc into back bar of center dc of petal of next flower, 8ch, sc into back bar of center dc of next petal; rep from * until all the flowers have been joined, turn.

2nd row: 3ch (count as 1 dc) 1dc into back loop of each ch or sc to end of row, 1dc in last sc, turn.

3rd row: 4ch, *skip 1 st, 1dc into next dc, 1ch; rep from * to last 2 dc, skip 1 dc, 1dc into top of tch.

Fasten off.

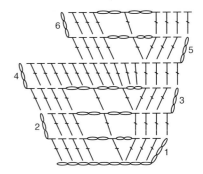

Filet Triangles

Worked lengthways.

1st row (right side): 12ch, 1dc into 4th ch from hook, 1dc in each of next 2 ch, 2ch, 1dc into same ch as last dc, 2ch, skip 2 ch, 1dc into each of next 4 ch, turn.

2nd row: 3ch (count as 1 dc), 1dc into each of next 3 dc, [2ch, 1dc into next dc] twice, 1dc in each of next 2 dc, 1dc into top of tch, turn.

3rd row: 3ch (count as 1 dc), 1dc into each of next 3 dc, 2ch, 1dc into same st as last dc, [2ch, 1dc into next dc] twice, 1dc in each of next 2 dc, 1dc into top of tch, turn.

4th row: 3ch (count as 1 dc), 1dc into each of next 3 dc, [2dc into next sp, 1dc into next dc] 3 times, 1dc in each of next 2 dc, 1dc into top of tch, turn.

5th row: 3ch (count as 1 dc), 1dc into each of next 3 dc, 2ch, 1dc into same st as last dc, 2ch, skip 2 dc, 1dc in each of next 4 dc, turn.

Rep 2nd to 5th rows until required length is reached, ending with a 4th row.

Fasten off.

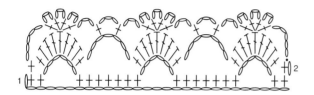

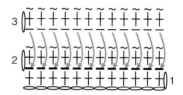

Three-picot Feathers

Multiple of 10 sts + 7 sts (add 1 st for base chain).

1st row (wrong side): 1sc into 2nd ch from hook, 1sc into next ch, 6ch, skip 3 ch, *1sc into each of next 7ch, 6ch, skip 3 ch; rep from * to last 2 ch, 1sc into each of last 2 ch, turn.

2nd row: 1ch, 1sc into first sc, *into next 6ch-arch work (1sc, 1hdc, 5dc, 1hdc, 1sc)**, 7ch; rep from * ending last rep at **, work 1sc into last sc, turn.

3rd row: 5ch, skip first 5 sts, work 1sc into next dc, [3ch, 1sc] 3 times into same st as last sc, *3ch, (1sc, 3ch, 1sc) into next 7ch-arch, 3ch, skip next 4 sts, 1sc into next dc, [3ch, 1sc] 3 times into same st as last sc; rep from * to last 5 sts, 5ch, sl st into last sc.

Fasten off.

Double Corded Edging

Multiple of any number of sts. (add 1 st for base chain)

Special abbreviation: reverse sc = working from left to right, 1sc into st loop specified of the st to the right, keeping the working yarn to the left of the hook.

1st row (right side): 1sc into 2nd ch from hook, work 1sc into each ch or equivalent interval to end. Do not turn.

2nd row: 1ch, *1 reverse sc back under front loop only of next st to right; rep from * to end.

Fasten off. Do not turn.

Rejoin yarn into left edge though back loop of first st.

3rd row: 1ch, *1 reverse sc back under back loop only of next st to right; rep from * to end.

Fasten off.

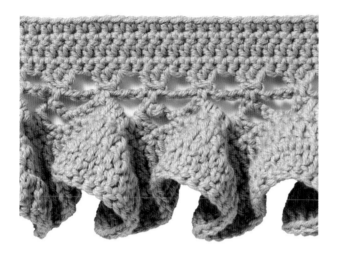

Scroll Ruffle

Multiple of 7 sts + 6 sts (add 1 st for base chain).

Special abbreviations: dc2tog = work 1dc into next 2 sts indicated leaving 1 loop of each on hook, yo and draw through all 3 loops on hook; **dc3tog** = work 1dc into next 3 sts indicated leaving 1 loop of each on hook, yo and draw through all 4 loops on hook.

1st row (right side): Skip 2 ch (count as 1 hdc), 1hdc into next ch, 1hdc into each ch to end, turn.

2nd row: 1ch, 1sc into each st to end, turn.

3rd row: 2ch (count as 1 hdc), 1hdc into each sc to end, turn. Rep 2nd row.

5th row: 3ch, skip first sc, 1dc into next sc, *3ch, skip 1 sc, dc3tog into next 3 sts; rep from * to last 3 sts, 3ch skip 1 st, dc2tog into next 2 sts, turn.

6th row: 1ch, 1sc into first st, 7ch, *1sc in next dc3tog, 7ch; rep to last dc, 1sc into top of tch, turn.

7th row: 3ch, (2dc, 3ch, 3dc) into next 7ch-sp, *2ch, 1sc into next 7ch-sp, 2ch, (3dc, 3ch 3dc) into next 7ch-sp; rep from * to end, turn.

8th row: 1ch, *1sc in each of next 3 dc, 5sc in next 3ch-sp, 1sc in each of next 3 dc**, 2sc in next 2ch-sp, skip next sc, 2sc in next 2ch-sp; rep from * ending last rep at ** with last dc in top of tch, turn.

9th row: 4ch, 1tr in each of next 2 sc, place st marker, *2dc into each of next 5 sc, place st marker**, 1tr in each of next 10 sc; rep from * ending last rep at **, 1tr in last 3 sts, turn. On foll row, work 2tr into each tr between st markers.

10th row: 4ch, 1tr in each of next 2 tr, *2tr in each of next 10 tr**, 1dc into each of next 10 tr; rep from * ending last rep at **, tr in next 2 tr, tr in top of tch, turn. Fasten off.

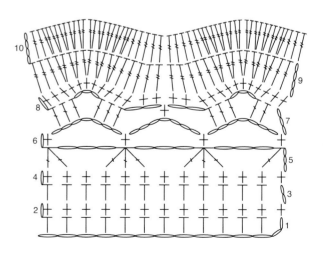

Zinnia Zigzag

(1 motif for each repeat).

Special abbreviations: 4ch-picot = 4ch, sl st in first ch for picot; **3ch-picot** = 3ch, sl st in first ch for picot.

Note: join the motifs by the 3ch-picots at the tip of the leaves progressing from right to left.

First motif

Base ring: 8ch, join with sl st to form ring.

1st round: 3ch (counts as 1dc), 1dc in ring, [4ch-picot, 2dc in ring] 8 times, 4ch picot, join with sl st to top of 3ch, 5ch, *5ch, 3ch-picot, 2ch, skip 1 ch, 1dc into next ch, 1tr in next 2 ch, 1dc into foll ch**, sl st into next ch; rep from * ending last rep at **, sl st into base of last leaf.
Fasten off.

Second motif

Base ring: 8ch, join with sl st to form ring.

1st round: 3ch (counts as 1dc), 1dc in ring, [4ch-picot, 2dc in ring] 8 times, 4ch picot, join with sl st to top of 3ch, 10ch, 3ch-picot, 2ch, skip 1 ch, 1dc into next ch, 1tr in next 2 ch, 1dc into foll ch, sl st into next ch, 5ch, 2ch drop loop from hook, insert hook in picot at tip of leaf of last motif and in dropped loop, draw loop through, 1ch, complete 3ch-picot, 1ch, skip 1 ch, 1dc into next ch, 1tr in next 2 ch, 1dc into foll ch, sl st into base of last leaf.
Fasten off.

Rep Second Motif until required length is reached.

Odd-ball Edge

Multiple of 8 sts + 7 sts (add 1 st for base chain).

Special abbreviations: beg-popcorn = work 7dc into indicated sp, remove hook from working loop, insert hook under top loops of tch, hook the working loop and draw this through the top loops to draw the popcorn closed, ch1; **8dc-popcorn** = work 8dc into indicated sp, remove hook from working loop, insert hook under top loops of first of the dc sts just worked, hook the working loop and draw this through the top loops to draw the popcorn closed, ch1.

Motif

Base ring: 5ch, join with sl st.

1st round: 1ch, 12sc into ring, sl st to first sc.

2nd round: Working into back loop only of each sc, 12ch, sl st into first sc, *sl st into next sc, 12ch, sl st into same sc; rep from * to end, sl st to first sc.

3rd round: Working into front loop only of each sc in 1st round, 8ch, sl st into first sc, *sl st into next sc, 8ch, sl st into same sc; rep from * to end, sl st to first sc.
Fasten off.

Header

1st row (right side): 1sc into 2nd ch from hook. 1sc into each ch to end, turn.

2nd row: 2ch, work 1hdc into each st to end, turn. Rep 2nd row once more.

4th row: 1ch, 1sc into first st, *4ch, skip 1 hdc, 1sc into next hdc; rep from * to end.

5th row: 3ch, beg-popcorn into next 4ch-sp, *3ch, in next 4ch-sp (1dc, 2ch, 1dc), 3ch, in next 4ch-sp 8dc-popcorn, 3ch, in next 4ch-sp (1dc, 2ch join to any 12-ch loop of next motif, 2 ch, sl st into the first ch from the header, 1dc), 3ch, in next 4ch-sp 8dc-popcorn; rep from * to end. Fasten off.

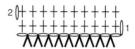

Slip Stitch Strands

Multiple of any number of sts.

Note: wrap yarn around a piece of card, cutting the yarn along one edge to create strands.

Foundation chain: 1ch, *place the center of a folded strand over the hook, and draw through the loop on the hook, 1ch using the working yarn; rep from * to required edging length, turn.

1st row: 1ch, *skip ch made with the strand, insert hook under and around next ch and complete a sc; rep from * to last ch, 1sc into last ch, turn.

2nd row: 1ch, 1 sc into each stitch to end.
Fasten off.
Pull all the strands tight and dcim the ends.

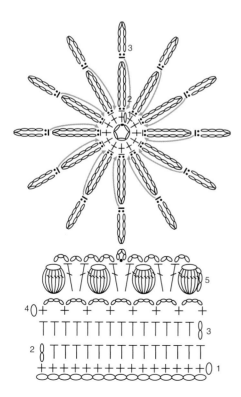

On the Fold

Multiple of 14 sts + 2 sts (add 1 st for base chain).
(1 motif for each repeat).

Motif

Base ring: 4ch, join with sl st.

1st round: 4ch (count as 1 dc and 1 ch), [1dc into ring, 1ch] 7 times, sl st to 3rd ch of tch. (8 spaces)

2nd round: 1ch, 1sc into same place as 1ch, [3ch, skip 1ch, 1sc into next dc] 8 times omitting sc at end of last rep, sl st to first sc.

3rd round: Sl st into each of next 2 ch, 1ch, 1sc into same space as 1ch, [6ch, 1sc into next 3ch-sp] 8 times omitting sc at end of last rep, sl st to first sc.

4th round: Sl st into each of next 3 ch, 1ch, 1sc into same space as 1ch, [6ch, 1sc into next 6ch-sp] 8 times omitting sc at end of last rep, sl st to first sc.

5th round: 1ch, 1sc into first sc, *(2dc, 4ch, 2dc) into next sp, 1sc into next sc; rep from * 7 more times omitting sc at end of last rep, sl st to first sc. Fasten off.

Header

1st row (right side): 1sc into 2nd ch from hook, work 1sc into each ch to end, turn.

Hold the motif with wrong side facing and the motif towards the back, begin at far right of the motif.

2nd row: 3ch (count as 1 dc) skip st at base of ch, 1dc into next st, using the diagram and the grey dots as a guide to st positions, work from right to left into the motif and the next st on the first row, *1dc into next 3 sts, 1dc into ch-sp, 1dc into next 4 sts indicated, 1dc into ch-sp, 1dc into each of last 3 sts indicated, 1 dc into next 2 sts on first row; rep from * across each motif to end.

3rd row: 2ch, work 1hdc into each st to end, turn.

4th row: 2ch, work 1hdc into back bar (below top loops) of each st to end.

Fasten off.

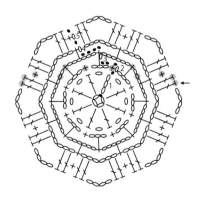

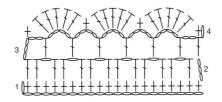

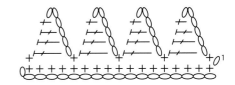

Hardy Edge

Multiple of 6 sts + 2 sts (add 1 st for base chain).

1st row (wrong side): 1sc into 2nd ch from hook, work 1sc into each ch to end, turn.

2nd row: 3ch (count as 1dc), skip first sc, 1dc into next sc, *1ch, skip 1 sc, 1dc into each of next 2 sc; rep from * to end, turn.

3rd row: 5ch (count as 1dc, 2 ch), 1dc into next ch-sp, *4ch, 1sc into next ch-sp; rep from * to last 2 sts, 2ch, 1dc into 3rd ch of tch, turn.

4th row: 1ch, 1sc into first dc, *work 5dc into next 4ch-sp, 1sc into next 4ch-sp; rep from * to end, placing last sc into 3rd ch of tch.

Fasten off.

Little Triangle Points

Multiple of 4 sts + 1 st (add 1 st for base chain).

Special abbreviation: pyramid = 6ch, 1sc into 3rd ch from hook, 1dc into each of next 3ch.

Note: work foundation row if working from a base chain.

Foundation row: 1sc into 2nd ch from hook and each ch to end, turn.

1st row (right side): 1ch, 1sc into first st, or join into an edge, 1ch, 1sc into starting point; counting either sts or equivalent interval, *work a pyramid, skip 3 sts, 1sc into next st; rep from * to end.

Fasten off.

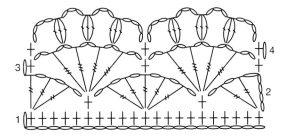

Papyrus Fans

Multiple of 10 sts + 1 st (add 1 st for base chain).
Special abbreviation: bobble = work 3dc into next space leaving 1 loop of each on hook, yo and through all 4 loops on hook.

1st row (wrong side): 1sc into 2nd ch from hook, work 1sc into each ch to end, turn.
2nd row: 5ch (count as 1tr, 1 ch), work [1tr, 1ch] twice into first sc, skip 4 sc, 1sc into next sc, *1ch, skip 4 sc, into next sc work [1tr, 1ch] 5 times, skip 4 sc, 1sc into next sc; rep from * to last 5 sc, 1ch, skip 4 sc, work 1tr into last sc, 1ch, into same st as last tr work (1tr, 1ch, 1tr), turn.

3rd row: 1ch, 1sc into first tr, *2ch, into next sc work [1dtr, 2ch] 4 times, skip 2 tr, 1sc into next tr; rep from * to end, placing last sc into 4th ch of tch, turn.
4th row: 1ch, 1sc into first sc, *4ch, skip next sp, 1 bobble into next 2ch-sp, [3ch, 1 bobble into next 2ch-sp] twice, 4ch, 1sc into next sc; rep from * to end.
Fasten off.

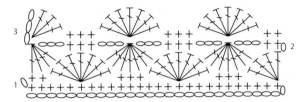

Catherine Wheels

Multiple of 10 sts + 6 sts (add 1 st for base chain).

Special abbreviation: cluster = work (yo, insert hook, yo, draw loop through, yo, draw through 2 loops) over the number of sts indicated, yo, draw through all loops on hook.

Note: work foundation row if working from a base chain.

Foundation row: 1sc into 2nd ch from hook and each ch to end, turn.

1st row (wrong side): 1ch, 1sc into first 2 sts, *skip 3 sts, 7dc into next st, skip 3 sts, 1sc into each of next 3 sts; rep from * to last 4 sts, skip 3 sts, 4dc into last ch, turn.

2nd row: 1ch, 1sc into first st, 1sc into next st, *3ch, 1 cluster over next 7 sts, 3ch, 1sc into each of next 3 sts; rep from * to last 4 sts, 3ch, 1 cluster over last 4 sts, skip tch, turn.

3rd row: 3ch (count as 1dc), 3dc into first st, *skip 3 ch, 1sc into each of next 3 sc, skip 3 ch, 7dc into loop that closed next cluster; rep from * to end in last cluster; skip 3 ch, 1sc into each of last 2 sc, skip tch.
Fasten off.

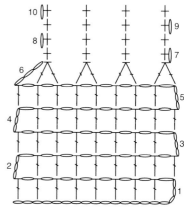

Filet Ruffle

Multiple of 4 sts + 1 st (add 3 sts for base chain).

Special abbreviation: dc2tog = work 1dc into next 2 ch or sts indicated leaving 1 loop of each on hook, yo and through all 3 loops on hook.

1st row (right side): Skip 5 ch (count as 1 dc, 1 ch) and 1dc into next ch, *1ch, skip 1 ch, 1dc into next ch; rep from * to end, turn.

2nd row: 4ch (count as 1 dc, 1 ch), 1dc into next dc, *1ch, 1dc into next dc; rep from * to end, turn.

Rep 2nd row 3 more times.

6th row: 3ch, *dc2tog in next 2 dc; rep from * to end, 2nd dc of last dc2tog worked into 3rd ch of tch, turn.

7th row: 1ch, 1sc into each st to last dc2tog, do not sc into tch, turn.

8th row: 1ch, 1sc into each st to end, turn.

Rep 8th row twice more.

Fasten off.

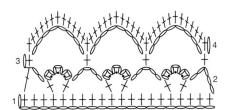

Picot Sprigs

Multiple of 6 sts + 2 sts (add 1 st for base chain).

Special abbreviation: picot = make 3 ch, sl st into 3rd ch from hook.

1st row (wrong side): 1sc into 2nd ch from hook, work 1sc into each ch to end, turn.

2nd row: 5ch (count as 1dc, 2 ch), skip first 3 sc, 1sc into next sc, work 3 picots, 1sc into next sc, *5ch, skip 4 sc, 1sc into next sc, work 3 picots, 1sc into next sc; rep from * to last 3 sc, 2ch, 1dc into last sc, turn.

3rd row: 1ch, 1sc into first dc, *8ch, 1sc into next 5ch-arch; rep from * to end, placing last sc into 3rd ch of tch, turn.

4th row: 1ch, 1sc into first sc, *11sc into next 8ch-arch, 1sc into next sc; rep from * to end.

Fasten off.

Beaded Loops

Multiple of 3 sts.

Note: thread beads onto yarn before starting.

Foundation chain (wrong side): 3ch, *slide 3 beads to base of hook, 3ch; rep from * until required length is reached, turn.

1st row: 1ch, 1sc into front loop of 2nd ch from hook, 1sc through front loop of each ch to end.

Fasten off.

3rd row: 5ch, skip first sc and next 5 dc, *1sc into next dc, 5ch, skip 1 dc, 1sc into next dc, ** 5ch, skip (next 5 dc, 1 sc and 5 dc); rep from * ending last rep at **, skip next 5 dc, 4ch, 1sc into last sc.

Fasten off.

Tassel

Using a piece of thick card slightly deeper than the required tassel, wrap yarn round the card until required tassel thickness is reached. Note the number of wraps made. Cut the yarn along one edge to create strands, fold the bunch of strands in half and loop through the arch from the right side to the wrong side. Pass the ends through the loop created in the middle of the strands, neaten the strand loop and gently pull the ends to tighten the loop. Trim the ends.

Rep for each tassel, duplicating the number of wraps each time.

Fringed Arches

Multiple of 9 sts + 1 st (add 1 st for base chain).

1st row (wrong side): 1sc into 2nd ch from hook, *3ch, skip 3 ch, 1sc into next ch, 7ch, 1sc into next ch, 3ch, skip 3 ch, 1sc into next ch; rep from * to end, turn.

2nd row: 1ch, 1sc into first sc, *skip 3 ch, work 13dc into next 7ch-arch, skip 3 ch, 1sc into next st; rep from * to end, skip tch, turn.

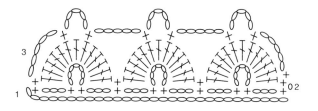

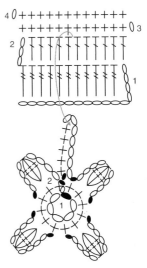

Floral Fringe

Multiple of 6 sts (add 3 sts for base chain).

(1 less motif than number of repeats on the header).

Special abbreviation: bobble = 3tr into next sc leaving 1 loop of each on hook, yo and draw through all 4 loops on hook.

Motif

Base ring: 5ch, join with a sl st.

1st round: 1ch, 12sc into ring, sl st into first sc.

2nd round: *4ch, 1 bobble into next sc, 4ch, sl st into each of next 2 sc; rep from * 3 more times, skipping 1 sl st at end of last rep, 7ch, 1sc into 3rd ch from hook, 1sc into each of next 4ch, sl st into first sc on first round. Fasten off.

Header

1st row: Skip 4 ch, work 1tr into next ch from hook, work 1tr in each ch to end, turn.

2nd row: 3ch (count as 1 dc), 1dc in each of next 5 tr; *drop loop from hook, insert hook through picot at end of stem of first motif and in dropped loop, draw loop through, 1dc in each of the next 6 tr; rep from * to end, turn.

3rd and 4th rows: 1ch, work 1sc into each st to end, turn. Fasten off.

Bell Ruffle

Multiple of 6 sts + 1 st (add 1 st for base chain).

Special abbreviations: dc/rf (raised double crochet at the front of the fabric) = yo, insert hook from in front and from right to left around the stem of the appropriate stitch, and complete stitch normally; **dc/rb** (raised double crochet at the back of the fabric) = yo, insert hook from behind and from right to left around the stem of the appropriate stitch, and complete stitch normally.

1st row (right side): Skip 2 ch, (count as 1 hdc), 1 hdc into next ch1, 1 hdc into each ch to end, turn.

2nd row: 2ch, *1 dc/rf around next st, 1 dc/rb around next st; rep from * to last 2 hdc, 1 dc/rf around next st, 1 hdc into top of tch, turn.

3rd row: 2ch, *1 dc/rb around next st, 1 dc/rf around next st; rep from * to last 2 sts, 1 dc/rb around next st, 1 hdc into top of tch, turn.

4th row: 2ch, *[1 dc/rf around next st, 1 dc/rb around next st] twice, 1 dc/rf around next st, 1ch, 3hdc into next st, 1ch rep from * to last 6 sts, [1 dc/rf around next st, 1 dc/rb around next st] twice, 1 dc/rf around next st, 1 hdc into top of tch, turn.

5th row: 2ch *[1 dc/rb around next st, 1 dc/rf around next st] twice, 1 dc/rb around next st, 1ch, 1 hdc into next ch-sp, 1 hdc into each of next 3 hdc, 1 hdc into next ch-sp; rep from * to last 6 sts, [1 dc/rb around next st, 1 dc/rf around next st] twice, 1 dc/rb around next st, 1 hdc into top of tch, turn.

6th row: 2ch, *[1dc/rf around next st, 1dc/rb around next st] twice, 1dc/rf around next st, 1ch, 1hdc into next ch-sp, 1hdc into each of next 5 hdc, 1hdc into next ch-sp; rep from * to last 6 sts, [1dc/rf around next st, 1dc/rb around next st] twice, 1dc/rf around next st, 1hdc into top of tch, turn.

7th row: 2ch, *[1dc/rb around next st, 1dc/rf around next st] twice, 1dc/rb around next st, 1ch, 1hdc into next ch-sp, 1hdc into each of next 7 hdc, 1hdc into next ch-sp; rep from * to last 6 sts, [1dc/rb around next st, 1dc/rf around next st] twice, 1dc/rb around next st, 1hdc into top of tch, turn.

8th row: 2ch, *[1dc/rf around next st, 1dc/rb around next st] twice, 1dc/rf around next st, 1ch, 1hdc into next ch-sp, 1hdc into each of next 9 hdc, 1hdc into next ch-sp; rep from * to last 6 sts, [1dc/rf around next st, 1dc/rb around next st] twice, 1dc/rf around next st, 1hdc into top of tch, turn.
Fasten off.

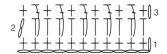

Two-tone Braid

Multiple of 2 sts + 1 st (add 1 st for base chain).

1st row (right side): 1sc into 2nd ch from hook, work 1sc into each ch to end, turn.

2nd row: 2ch, 1hdc into each st to end, turn.
Fasten off yarn A, join in yarn B.

3rd row: 1ch, 1 sc into first st, *skip 1 hdc from row 2, 1dc into equivalent sc on 1st row, 1sc into next st in row 2; rep from * to end.
Fasten off.

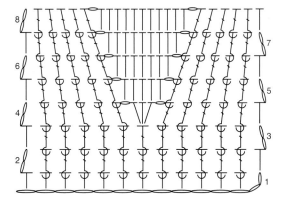

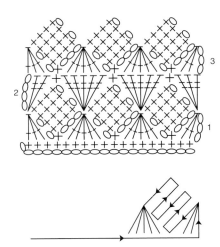

Diamonds and Fans

Multiple of 6 sts (add 1 st for base chain).

Special abbreviations: dc2tog = work 1dc into each of next 2 sts leaving 1 loop of each on hook, yo and through all 3 loops on hook; **cluster** = work 1dc into each of next 5 sts leaving 1 loop of each on hook, yo and through all 6 loops on hook; **half cluster** = work 1dc into each of next 3 sts leaving 1 loop of each on hook, yo and through all 4 loops on hook.

Note: work foundation row if working from a base chain.

Foundation row: 1sc into 2nd ch from hook and each ch to end, turn.

1st row (right side): 3ch (counts as dc), or join into an edge, 3ch; counting either sts or equivalent interval, work dc2tog working into first 2 sts, *3ch, 1sc into next st, turn, 1ch, 1sc into last sc worked, 3sc into last 3ch-sp formed,

[turn, 1ch, 1sc into each of the 4 sc] 3 times, work 1 cluster over next 5 sts; rep from * to end, working half cluster at end of last rep, turn.

2nd row: 4ch (count as 1tr), work 2tr into top of first half cluster, skip 3 sc, 1sc into next sc, *5tr into top of next cluster, skip 3 sc, 1sc into next sc; rep from * to last dc2tog, 3tr into top of tch, turn.

3rd row: 3ch (count as 1dc), skip first tr, work dc2tog over next 2 tr, *3ch, 1sc into next sc, turn, 1ch, 1sc into last sc worked, 3sc into last 3ch-sp formed, [turn, 1ch, 1sc into each of the 4 sc] 3 times, work 1 cluster over next 5tr; rep from * to end, and working half cluster at end of last rep placing last dc of half cluster into top of tch.

Fasten off.

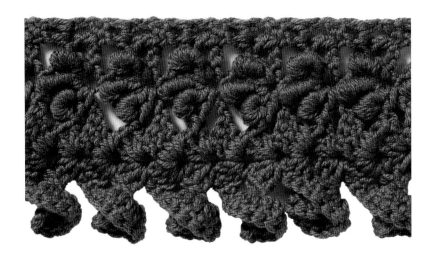

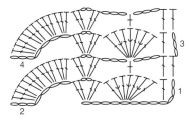

Bullion Scrolls

Worked lengthways over 10 sts (add 2 sts for base chain).
Special abbreviations: bullion stitch = yo hook, 10 times, insert hook into ch or st indictated, yo, ease the loop through all the loops on hook, 1 ch; **bullion group** = work 1 dc, [1 bullion st, 1 dc] 3 times, into ch or st indicated; **shell** = work 3 dc, 2 ch, 3 dc, into ch or st indicated.

1st row (right side): Skip 3 ch (count as 1 dc), 1 dc into next ch, skip 3 ch, work a bullion group into next ch, skip 3 ch, work a shell into last ch, turn.

2nd row: 7 ch, 3 dc into 4th ch from hook, 3 dc into each of next 3 ch, shell into 2 ch-sp at center of next shell, 3 ch, 1 sc into 2nd bullion at center of next group, 3 ch, skip next 3 sts, 1 dc into next dc, 1 dc into top of tch, turn.

3rd row: 3 ch (count as 1 dc), skip first st, 1 dc into next st, skip 3 ch, bullion group into next sc, skip 3 ch, shell into 2 ch-sp at center of next shell, turn.

Rep 2nd and 3rd rows until required length is reached, ending with a 2nd row.
Fasten off.

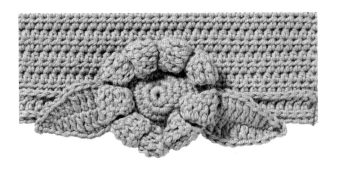

Curling Petals

(1 motif for each repeat).

Note: pattern is worked in a spiral, do not join at the end of 1st to 6th rounds. The leaves are from the Leaf Layer edging on page 95, with the round of picots omitted.

Base ring: 6ch, join with sl st.

1st round: 8sc into ring.

2nd round: 3sc in each st. (24 sts)

3rd and 4th rounds: 1sc in each st.

5th round: *1sc in next sc, 2sc in next sc; rep from * around. (36 sts)

6th round: 1sc in each st.

7th round: *9ch, sl st in 2nd ch from hook, 1sc in next ch, 1dc in each of next 3 ch, 1tr in each of next 3 ch, skip next 3 sts of previous round, sl st in next st; rep from * around, join with sl st. (9 petals)

Slip stitch motifs to fabric.

Fasten off.

Arching Spans

Multiple of 7 sts + 1 st (add 2 sts for base chain).

1st row (right side): Skip 3 ch (count as 1dc) and 1dc into next ch, work 1dc into each ch to end, turn.

2nd row: 1ch, 1sc into each of first 2 dc, *7ch, skip 4 dc, 1sc into each of next 3 dc, rep from * to end, omitting 1sc at end of last rep and placing last sc into top of tch, turn.

3rd row: 1ch, 1sc into each of first 2 sc, *7sc into 7ch-arch, 1sc into each of next 3 sc, rep from * to end, omitting 1sc at end of last rep, turn.

4th row: 7ch (count as 1tr, 3 ch), skip first 4 sc, 1sc into each of next 3 sc, *7ch, skip 7 sc, 1sc into each of next 3 sc; rep from * to last 4 sc, 3ch, 1tr into last sc, turn.

5th row: 1ch, 1sc into tr, 3sc into first arch, 1sc into each of next 3 sc, *7sc into next 7ch-arch, 1sc into each of next 3 sc; rep from * to last arch, 3sc into last arch, 1sc into 4th ch of tch.

Fasten off.

Picots with Chain Texture

Multiple of 12 sts + 11 sts (add 1 st for base chain).
Note: work foundation row if working from a base chain.

Foundation row: 1sc into 2nd ch from hook and each ch to end, turn.

1st row (right side): 1ch, 1sc into first st, or join into an edge, 1ch, 1sc into starting point; counting either sts or equivalent interval, [5ch, skip 4 ch, 1sc into next ch] twice, *[5ch, 1sc into next ch] twice, [5ch, skip 4 ch, 1sc into next ch] twice; rep from * to end, turn.

2nd row: 6ch (count as 1dc, 3 ch), 1sc into first 5ch-arch, *3ch, 1sc into next 5ch-arch; rep from * to end, 3ch, 1dc into last sc, turn.

3rd row: 1ch, 1sc into first dc, *5ch, skip 3ch-arch, 1sc into next 3ch-arch, into same arch as last sc work [5ch, 1sc] twice, 5ch, skip 3ch-arch, 1sc into next 3ch-arch; rep from * to end, working last sc into 3rd ch of tch.
Fasten off.

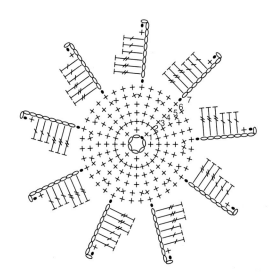

Curling Petals

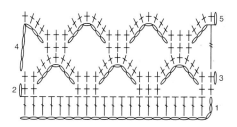

Arching Spans

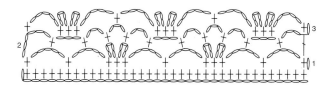

Picots with Chain Texture

Romanesque Arches

Multiple of 10 sts + 1 st (add 1 st for base chain).

1st row (right side): 1sc into 2nd ch from hook, work 1sc into each ch to end, turn.

2nd row: 3ch (count as 1dc), skip first sc, 1dc into each of next 3 sc, *3ch, skip 3 sc, 1dc into each of next 7 sc; rep from * to end, omitting 3dc at end of last rep, turn.

3rd row: 1ch, 1sc into each of first 4 dc, 3sc into next 3ch-sp, *1sc into each of next 7 dc, 3sc into next 3ch-sp; rep from * to last 4dc, 1sc into each of next 3 dc, 1sc into 3rd ch of tch, turn.

4th row: 1ch, 1sc into first sc, 2ch, skip 2 sc, 1sc into next sc, 8ch, skip 3 sc, 1sc into next sc, *5ch, skip 5 sc, 1sc into next sc, 8ch, skip 3 sc, 1sc into next sc; rep from * to last 3 sc, 2ch, 1sc into last sc, turn.

5th row: 1ch, 1sc into first sc, 19dc into 8ch-arch, *1sc into next 5ch-sp, 19dc into next 8ch-arch; rep from * to last 2ch-sp, 1sc into last sc.
Fasten off.

Raised-stitch Rib

Worked lengthways over any number of sts (add 2 sts for base chain).

Special abbreviation: dc/rf (raised double crochet at the front of the fabric) = yo, insert hook from in front and from right to left around the stem of the appropriate stitch, and complete stitch normally.

1st row: Skip 3 ch (count as 1 dc), 1dc into each ch to end, turn.

2nd row: 2ch, work 1 dc/rf around each st until tch, 1hdc into top of tch, turn.
Rep 2nd row until required length is reached.
Fasten off.

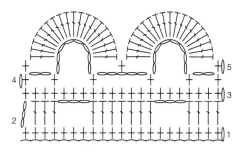

Romanesque Arches

Open Fans

Multiple of 10 sts + 1 st (add 1 st for base chain).

Special abbreviation: dc2tog = work 2dc into next 3ch-arch leaving 1 loop of each on hook, yo and through all 3 loops on hook.

1st row (wrong side): 1sc into 2nd ch from hook, *3ch, skip 3 ch, 1sc into next ch, 3ch, skip 1 ch, 1sc into next ch, 3ch, skip 3 ch, 1sc into next ch; rep from * to end, turn.

2nd row: 1ch, 1sc into first sc, *1ch, skip next 3ch-sp, dc2tog into next 3ch-arch, into same arch as last dc2tog work [3ch, dc2tog] 4 times, 1ch, skip next 3ch-sp, 1sc into next sc; rep from * to end, turn.

3rd row: 7ch (count as 1tr, 3 ch), skip next 3ch-arch, 1sc into next 3ch-arch, 3ch, 1sc into next 3ch-arch, 3ch, skip next 3ch-arch, 1tr into next sc, *3ch, skip next 3ch-arch, 1sc into next 3ch-arch, 3ch, 1sc into next 3ch-arch, 3ch, skip next 3ch-arch, 1tr into next sc; rep from * to end. Fasten off.

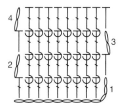

Raised-stitch Rib

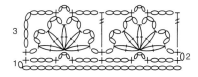

Open Fans

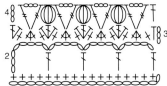

Puff Stitch Jewels

Multiple of 4 sts + 1 st (add 1 st for base chain).
Special abbreviations: sc3tog = work 1sc into next 3 ch or sts indicated leaving 1 loop of each on hook, yo and through all 4 loops on hook; **hdc5tog (puff stitch)** = work 5hdc into next st indicated, leaving 2 loops from each on hook (in other words, [yo, insert hook, yo, draw loop through] 5 times]) yo and through all 11 loops on hook.

1st row (right side): 1sc into 2nd ch from hook, work 1sc into each ch to end, turn.

2nd row: 8ch (count as 1dc and 5 ch), skip first 4 sts, 1dc into next st, *5ch, skip 3 sts, dc into next st; rep from * to end, turn.

3rd row: 3ch (count as 1dc), 1hdc into first st, *1sc into next ch, sc3tog over next 3 ch, 1sc into next ch, (1hdc, 1dc **, 1hdc) into next st; rep from * ending last rep at **, turn.

4th row: 3ch (count as 1dc), skip first 3 sts, *(1tr, 3ch, 1tr) into next sc3tog, skip 2 sts**, work hdc5tog into next dc; rep from * ending last rep at **, 1dc into top of tch. Fasten off.

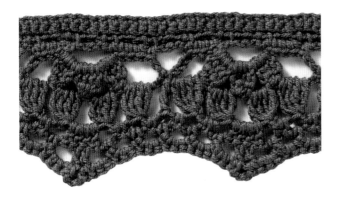

Grand Bobbles

Multiple of 16 sts + 1 st (add 1 st for base chain).

Special abbreviation: bobble = 4tr into arch leaving 1 loop of each on hook, yo and through all 5 loops on hook.

1st row (wrong side): 1sc into 2nd ch from hook, work 1sc into each ch to end, turn.

2nd row: 1ch, 1sc into first sc, *3ch, skip 3 sc, 1sc into next sc; rep from * to end, turn.

3rd row: 1ch, 1sc into first sc, 1ch, 1sc into first sp, *3ch, 1sc into next sp; rep from * to last sc, 1ch, 1sc into last sc, turn.

4th row: 6ch (count as 1dc, 3 ch), skip first sc, 1sc into next sc, 3sc into next 3ch-sp, 1sc into next sc, *6ch, 1sc into next sc, 3sc into next 3ch-sp, 1sc into next sc; rep from * to last sc, 3ch, 1dc into last sc, turn.

5th row: 1ch, 1sc into first dc, *4ch, work 1 bobble into next 6ch-arch, into same arch as last bobble work [3ch, 1 bobble] twice, 4ch, 1sc into next 6ch-arch; rep from * to end, placing last sc into 3rd ch of tch, turn.

6th row: 7ch (count as 1tr, 3 ch), *work 1 bobble into next 4ch-arch, 3ch, [1 bobble into next 3ch-arch, 3ch] twice, 1 bobble into next 4ch-arch, 3ch, 1tr into next sc, 3ch; rep from * to end, omitting 3ch at end of last rep, turn.

7th row: 1ch, 1sc into first tr, 1ch, [1sc into next arch, 3ch] twice, 4dc into next arch, *3ch, [1sc into next arch, 3ch] 4 times, 4dc into next arch; rep from * to last 2 arches, [3ch, 1sc into next arch] twice, 1ch, 1sc into 4th ch of tch, turn.

8th row: 1ch, 1sc into first sc, 3ch, [1sc into next 3ch-arch, 3ch] twice, skip 1 dc, 1dc into each of next 2 dc, *3ch, [1sc into next arch, 3ch] 5 times, skip 1 dc, 1dc into each of next 2 dc; rep from * to last 2 3ch-arches, 3ch, [1sc into next arch, 3ch] twice, 1sc into last sc, turn.

9th row: 1ch, 1sc into first sc, work 3sc into each of next 3 arches, 1sc into next dc, 3ch, 1sc into next dc, *3sc into each of next 6 arches, 1sc into next dc, 3ch, 1sc into next dc; rep from * to last 3 arches, 3sc into each of last 3 arches, 1sc into last sc.

Fasten off.

Beaded Triangles

Multiple of 6 sts + 1 st (add 1 st for base chain).

Special abbreviation: pb (place bead) = slide next bead along yarn to base of hook.

Note: thread beads onto yarn before starting.

1st row (right side): 1sc into 2nd ch from hook, work 1sc into each ch to end, turn.

2nd row: 1ch, 1sc into first sc, *[pb, 1ch] 6 times, work 1sc into 2nd ch from hook, then working 1 st into each of next 4ch work 1hdc, 1dc, 1tr and 1dtr, skip 5sc on previous row, 1sc into next sc; rep from * to end. Fasten off. Do not turn.

Rejoin yarn, with WS facing, in 3rd skipped sc under first triangle.

3rd row: 1ch, 1sc into 3rd skipped sc, *[pb, 1ch] 6 times, work 1sc into 2nd ch from hook, then working 1 st into each of next 4ch work 1hdc, 1dc, 1tr and 1dtr, skip 5sc on previous row, 1sc into next sc; rep from * to end to within last 3 sts.

Fasten off.

Zigzag Dainty

Multiple of 6 sts + 1 st (add 1 st for base chain).

Special abbreviation: bobble = work 3dtr into next st leaving 1 loop of each on hook, yo and through all 4 loops on hook.

1st row (right side): 1sc into 2nd ch from hook, work 1sc into each ch to end, turn.

2nd row: 8 ch (count as 1dc, 5 ch), skip first 6 sc, 1dc into next sc, *5ch, skip 5 sc, 1dc into next sc; rep from * to end, turn.

3rd row: 6ch (count as 1tr, 2 ch), work 1 bobble into first dc, *into next dc work (1 bobble, 5ch, 1 bobble); rep from * to last dc, into top of tch work (1 bobble, 2ch, 1tr), turn.

4th row: 1ch, 1sc into first tr, *7ch, 1sc into next 5ch-arch; rep from * to end, placing last sc into 4th ch of tch, turn.

5th row: 1ch, 1sc into first sc, *9sc into next 7ch-arch, 1sc into next sc; rep from * to end.

Fasten off.

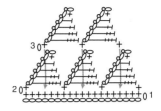

Beaded Triangles

Pintuck Ridges

Multiple of any number of sts (add 1 st for base chain).

1st row (wrong side): 1sc into 2nd ch from hook, 1sc into each ch to end, turn.

2nd row: 1ch, 1sc into front loop of each sc to end, turn.

3rd row: 1ch, 1sc into unworked top loop (now front loop) of each sc of first row, turn.

4th row: 1ch, 1sc into each sc of 3rd row to end, turn.

5th row: 1ch, 1sc into each sc to end, turn.

Rep 2nd to 5th rows twice more.

Fasten off.

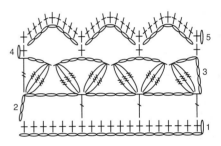

Zigzag Dainty

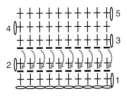

Pintuck Ridges

Heart Frill

Multiple of 3 sts + 2 sts (add 1 st for base chain).

Special abbreviations: picot = 6ch, 1sc in 4th ch from hook; **3tr-cluster** = yo twice, insert hook into same place as last sl st, yo and pull through, [yo and pull through 2 loops on hook] twice, [yo twice, insert hook into next tr, yo and pull through, (yo and pull through 2 loops on hook) twice] twice, yo and pull through last 4 loops on hook; **left-cluster** = [yo twice, insert hook into next tr, yo and pull through, (yo and pull through 2 loops on hook) twice] 3 times, yo twice, insert hook into same tr, yo and pull through, [yo and pull through 2 loops on hook] twice, yo and pull through last 5 loops on hook; **right-cluster** = yo twice, insert hook into next tr, yo and pull through, [yo and pull through 2 loops on hook] twice, yo twice, insert hook into same tr, yo and pull through, [yo and pull through 2 loops on hook] twice, [yo twice, insert hook into next tr, yo and pull through, (yo and pull through 2 loops on hook) twice], twice, yo and pull through last 5 loops on hook.

1st row (right side): 1sc into 2nd ch from hook, work 1sc into each ch to end, turn.

2nd row: 4ch (count as 1tr), 2tr into base of tch, *3ch, skip 2 sc, 3tr into next sc; rep from * to end of row, turn.

3rd row: 4ch (count as 1tr), 1tr into base of tch, *1tr into next tr, 2tr into next tr, picot, 2ch, 2tr into next tr; rep from * to last 2 tr, 1tr into next tr, 2tr into top of tch, turn.

4th row: 4ch (count as 1tr), 1tr into base of tch, *1tr into each of next 3tr, 2tr into next tr, 9ch, 2tr into next tr; rep from * to last 4 tr, 1tr into each of next 3tr, 2tr into top of tch, turn.

5th row: 4ch (count as 1tr), 3tr-cluster *5ch, 1sl st into next tr, 5ch, left-cluster, 6ch, skip 4 ch, (1sc, 4ch, 1sc) into next ch, 6ch, skip 4 ch, right-cluster; rep from * to last 4 tr, 5ch, 1 sl st into next tr, 5ch, 1 left-cluster over next 3 tr. Fasten off.

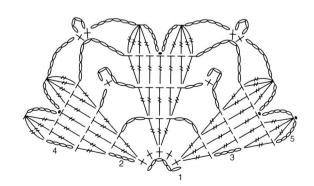

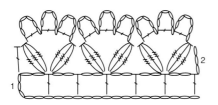

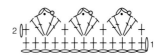

Crowned Zigzag

Multiple of 9 sts + 1 st (add 4 sts for base chain).

Special abbreviation: bobble = work 3dtr into next st leaving one loop of each on hook, yo and through all 4 loops on hook.

1st row (wrong side): Skip 7 ch (count as 1dc, 2ch) and 1dc into next ch, *2ch, skip 2 ch, 1dc into next ch; rep from * to end, turn.

2nd row: 3ch (count as 1dc), skip next sp, work 1 bobble into next sp, [6ch, 1dc into first of these ch] 3 times, 1 bobble into same sp as last bobble, *skip 2 sps, work 1 bobble into next sp, [6ch, 1dc into first of these ch] 3 times, 1 bobble into same sp as last bobble; rep from * to last sp, skip 2 ch, 1dc into next ch.
Fasten off.

Shells with Bead Drops

Multiple of 5 sts (add 1 st for base chain).

Special abbreviation: pb (place bead) = slide next bead along yarn to base of hook.

Note: thread beads onto yarn before starting.

1st row (right side): 1sc into 2nd ch from hook, work 1sc into each ch to end, turn.

2nd row: 1ch, 1sc in first st, *skip 2 sc, (2dc, 2ch, pb, sl st into 2nd ch from hook, 2dc) into next sc, skip 1 sc, sc into next sc; rep from * to end.
Fasten off.

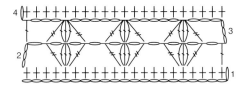

Diamond Braid

Multiple of 6 sts + 3 sts (add 1 st for base chain).

Special abbreviations: bobble = work 3dc into next st leaving 1 loop of each on hook, yo and through all 4 loops on hook; **cluster** = work 1tr into next ch-sp leaving 2 loops on hook, 3dc into top of next bobble leaving 1 loop of each on hook (5 loops on hook), skip 1ch sp, 1tr into next ch-sp leaving 6 loops on hook, yo and through all 6 loops on hook.

1st row (wrong side): 1sc into 2nd ch from hook, work 1sc into each ch to end, turn

2nd row: 4ch (count as 1dc, 1 ch), skip first 4 sc, 1tr into next sc, work (1ch, 1 bobble, 1ch, 1tr) into same st as last tr, 1ch, *skip 5 sc, 1tr into next sc, work (1ch, 1 bobble, 1ch, 1tr) into same st as last tr, 1ch; rep from * to last 4 sc, 1dc into last sc, turn.

3rd row: 6ch (count as 1dc, 3 ch), *1 cluster, 5ch; rep from * to end, working first tr of each cluster into same ch-sp as last tr of previous cluster and omitting 2ch at end of last rep, 1dc into 3rd ch of tch, turn.

4th row: 1ch, 1sc into first dc, 3sc into first 3ch-sp, 1sc into top of first cluster, *5sc into next 5ch-sp, 1sc into top of next cluster; rep from * to last sp, 3sc into last sp, 1sc into 3rd ch of tch.

Fasten off.

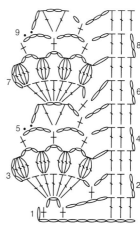

Pineapple Edge

Worked lengthways over 10 sts (add 1 for base chain).

Special abbreviation: 4dc-bobble = work 4dc into next st leaving 1 loop of each on hook, yo and through all 5 loops on hook.

1st row (wrong side): Skip 1 ch, 1sc into next ch, 3ch, skip 1 ch, 1sc into next ch, 4ch, skip 4 ch, 1dc in each of next 3 ch, turn.

2nd row: 3ch (counts as dc), skip first dc, 1dc in each of the next 2 dc, 2ch, 1sc into 4ch-sp, 1ch, 7dc into 3ch-sp, turn.

3rd row: 3ch, 4dc-bobble into first dc, [3ch, skip 1 dc, 4dc-bobble into next dc] 3 times, 1ch, skip next 2ch-sp, 1dc in each of next 2 dc, 1dc into top of tch, turn.

4th row: 3ch (counts as dc), skip first dc, 1dc into each of next 2 dc, 2ch, 1sc into next 3ch-sp, [4ch, 1sc in next 3ch-sp] twice, turn.

5th row: Sl st into each of next 2 ch, 2ch, 1dc into next sc, 2ch, 1dc into same st as last dc, 2ch, 1 sc into next ch-sp, 3ch, skip next 2ch-sp, 1dc in each of next 2 dc, 1dc into top of tch, turn.

6th row: 3ch (counts as dc), skip first dc, 1dc into each of next 2 dc, 2ch, skip next 3ch-sp, 1 sc into next 2ch-sp, 1ch, 7dc into 2ch-sp, turn.

Rep 3rd to 6th rows until required length is reached.

Fasten off

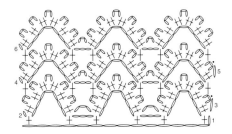

Fan Edge

Multiple of 8 sts + 1 st (add 4 sts for base chain).

1st row (right side): Skip 9 ch (count as 1dc, 3 ch) and 1dc into next ch, *3ch, skip 3 ch, 1dc into next ch; rep from * to end, working a multiple of 2 ch sps, turn.

2nd row: 1ch, 1sc into first dc, *2ch, into next dc work (3tr, 3ch, 3tr), 2ch, 1sc into next dc; rep from * to end, placing last sc into 4th ch of tch, turn.

3rd row: 1ch, 1sc into first sc, *5ch, 1sc into next 3ch-sp, 5ch, 1sc into next sc; rep from * to end, turn.

4th row: 1ch, 1sc into first sc, *4ch, 1sc into next sc; rep from * to end, turn.

5th row: 1ch, 1sc into first sc, *3ch, into next sc work (3tr, 3ch, 3tr), 3ch, 1sc into next sc; rep from * to end. Fasten off.

Crown Ruffle

Multiple of 5 sts + 4 sts (add 1 st for base chain).

1st row (right side): 1sc into 2nd ch from hook, *7ch, skip 2 ch, 1sc into next ch**, 3ch, skip 1 ch, 1sc into next ch; rep from * ending last rep at **, turn.

2nd row: 1ch, * work [2sc, 3ch] 5 times in next 7ch-sp, 2sc into the same 7ch-sp **, 3ch, skip next 3ch-sp; rep from * ending last rep at **, turn.

3rd row: 1ch, sl st into first ch-sp, 1sc into same ch-sp, *7ch, skip next 3 ch-sp, 1sc into next ch-sp**, 3ch, skip next ch-sp, 1sc into next ch-sp; rep from * ending last rep at **.

Rep 2nd and 3rd rows and then 2nd row once more. Fasten off.

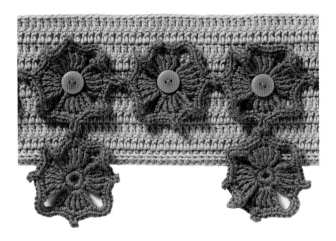

Applied Shamrock

(1 motif for each repeat).

First motif

Base ring: 9ch, join with sl st.

1st round: 1ch, 16sc into ring, sl st to first sc.

2nd round: 5ch (count as 1 tr), 2tr into same st as last sl st, 3tr into next sc, [7ch, skip 2 sc, 3tr into each of next 2 sc] 3 times, 7ch, sl st to top of tch.

3rd round: 1ch, 1sc into same st as last sl st, *1dc into next tr, 2dc into next tr, 4ch, sl st through top of last dc (picot), 2dc into next tr, 1dc into next tr, 1sc into next tr, 7sc into next 7ch-sp, 1sc into next tr; rep from * 3 times more, skipping 1sc at end of last rep, sl st to first sc. Fasten off.

Second motif

Base ring: 9ch, join with sl st.

1st round: 1ch, 16sc into ring, sl st to first sc.

2nd round: 5ch (count as 1 tr), 2tr into same st as last sl st, 3tr into next sc, [7ch, skip 2 sc, 3tr into each of next 2 sc] 3 times, 7ch, sl st to top of tch.

3rd round: 1ch, 1sc into same st as last sl st, *1dc into next tr, 2dc into next tr, 4ch, join motifs as folls, drop loop from hook, insert hook in far right picot of last motif and in dropped loop, draw loop through, 1ch, sl st through top of last dc, 2dc into next tr, 1dc into next tr, 1sc into next tr, 7sc into next 7ch-sp, 1sc into next tr; cont around same as first motif, skipping 1sc at end of last rep, sl st to first sc. Fasten off.

Rep Second Motif but joining through the lower picot of every second motif.

Position along an edge as shown in the photograph and whip stitch to secure.

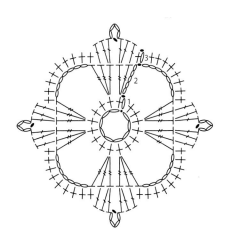

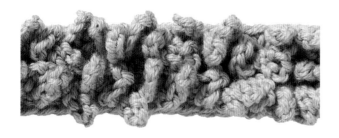 

Astrakhan Edge

Any number of sts (add 2 sts for base chain).

Note: work all rows with right side facing, i.e. work even-numbered rows from left to right.

1st row (right side): Skip 3 ch (count as 1dc) and 1dc into next ch, work 1dc into each ch to end. Do not turn.

2nd row: *7ch, sl st into front loop only of next dc to right; rep from * ending 7ch, sl st into top of tch at beg of row. Do not turn.

3rd row: 3ch (count as 1dc), skip st at base of ch, 1dc into back loop only of next and each st of second-to-last row to end. Do not turn.

Rep 2nd and 3rd rows until required depth is reached, ending with a 3rd row.

Finishing row: Turn, 2ch (counts as hdc), work 1hdc in each st to end.

Fasten off.

Bobble Delight

Multiple of 6 sts + 5 sts (add 1 st for base chain).

Special abbreviation: bobble = work 4dtr into ch leaving 1 loop of each on hook, yo and through all 5 loops on hook.

1st row (right side): 1sc into 2nd ch from hook, work 1sc into each ch to end, turn.

2nd row: 6ch (count as 1dc, 3 ch), skip first 4 sc, 1dc into next sc, *1ch, skip 1 sc, 1dc into next sc, 3ch, skip 3 sc, 1dc into next sc; rep from * to end, turn.

3rd row: 1ch, 1sc into first dc, *4ch, skip 1 ch, 1 bobble into next ch, 4ch, 1sc into next dc, 1ch, skip 1 ch, sc in next dc; rep from * to end, omitting last ch and sc and working final sc into 3rd ch of tch.

Fasten off.

Chain Wave

Multiple of 4 sts + 1 st (add 3 sts for base chain).

1st row (right side): Skip 5 ch (count as 1dc, 1ch) and 1dc into next ch or join into an edge and 3ch, counting either ch or equivalent interval, *1ch, skip 1 ch, 1dc into next ch; rep from * to end, turn.

2nd row: 1ch, 1sc into first dc, *5ch, skip 1 dc, 1sc into next dc; rep from * to last dc, 5ch, skip 1 dc and 1ch, 1sc into next ch, turn.

3rd row: 1ch, 1sc into first sc, work 7sc into each 5ch-arch to end, 1sc into last sc, turn.

4th row: 5ch (count as 1dc, 2 ch), skip first 4 sc, 1sc into next sc, *3ch, skip 6 sc, 1sc into next sc; rep from * to last 4 sc, 2ch, 1dc into last sc, turn.

5th row: 1ch, 1sc into first dc, 5ch, 1sc into 2ch-sp, into each sp work (1sc, 5ch, 1sc) to end, placing last sc into 3rd ch of tch.

Fasten off.

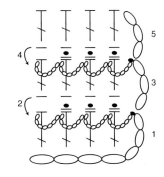

Astrakhan Edge

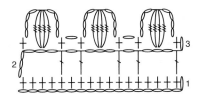

Bobble Delight

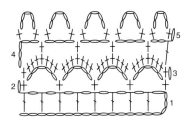

Chain Wave

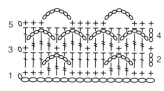

Relief Chain Arches

Multiple of 8 sts + 1 st (add 1 st for base chain).

1st row (wrong side): 1sc into 2nd ch from hook, 1sc into each of next 2 ch, *7ch, skip 3 ch**, 1sc into each of next 5 ch; rep from * ending last rep at ** when 3 ch remain, 1sc into each of last 3 ch, turn.

2nd row: 3ch (count as 1dc), skip st at base of ch, 1dc into each of next 2 sts, *going behind 7ch-loop work 1tr into each of next 3 base ch**, 1dc into each of next 5 sc; rep from * ending last rep at ** when 3 sts remain, 1dc into each of last 3 sts, skip tch, turn.

3rd row: 1ch, 1sc into first st, *7ch, skip 3 sts, 1sc into next st, at same time catching in 7ch-loop of second-to-last row, 7ch, skip 3 sts, 1sc into next st; rep from * to end, turn.

4th row: 3ch (count as 1dc), skip st at base of ch, *going behind 7ch-loop of last row work 1tr into each of next 3 sts of second-to-last row, 1dc into next sc; rep from * to end, skip tch, turn.

5th row: 1ch, 1sc into each of first 2 sts, *1sc into next st, at same time catching in 7ch-loop of second-to-last row, 7ch, skip 3 sts, 1sc into next st, at same time catching in center of 7ch-loop of second-to-last row**, 1sc into each of next 3 sts; rep from * ending last rep at ** when 2 sts remain, 1sc into each next st, 1 sc into tch.

Fasten off.

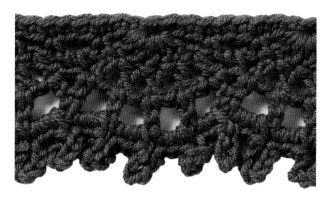

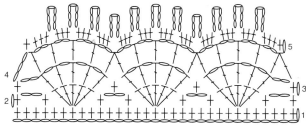

Peacock Fans

Multiple of 9 sts + 4 sts (add 1 st for base chain).

Special abbreviation: dc2tog = work 1dc into each of next 2 dc leaving 1 loop of each on hook, yo and through all 3 loops on hook.

1st row (right side): 1sc into 2nd ch from hook, work 1sc into each ch to end, turn.

2nd row: 1ch, 1sc into first sc, 2ch, skip 2 sc, 1sc into next sc, *skip 2 sc, 5dc into next sc, skip 2 sc, 1sc into next sc, 2ch, skip 2 sc, 1sc into next sc; rep from * to end, turn.

3rd row: 1ch, 1sc into first sc, 2ch, *1dc into next dc, [1ch, 1dc into next dc] 4 times**, 1sc into next 2ch-sp; rep from * ending last rep at **, 2ch, 1sc into last sc, turn.

4th row: 3 ch (count as 1dc), [1dc into next dc, 2ch] 4 times, *dc2tog, 2ch, [1dc into next dc, 2ch] 3 times; rep from * to last dc, work 1dc into next dc leaving 2 loops on hook, 1dc into last sc leaving 3 loops on hook, yo and through all 3 loops, turn.

5th row: 1ch, 1sc into first st, 3sc into first 2ch-sp, *7ch, 3sc into next 2ch-sp; rep from * to end, 1sc into top of tch. Fasten off.

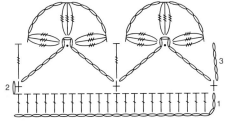

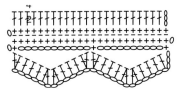

Bobble Sprigs

Multiple of 11 sts + 1 st (add 2 sts for base chain).

Special abbreviation: bobble = work 3dtr into 3ch loop leaving 1 loop of each on hook, yo and through all 4 loops on hook.

1st row (right side): Skip 3 ch (count as 1dc) and 1dc into next ch, work 1dc into each ch to end, turn.

2nd row: 1ch, 1sc into first dc, *9ch, sl st into 3rd ch from hook, 7ch, skip 10 dc, 1sc into next dc; rep from * to end, placing last sc into top of tch, turn.

3rd row: 5ch, *work 1 bobble into next 3ch-loop, 5ch, into same loop as last bobble work (1 bobble, 5ch, 1 bobble), 1dtr into next sc; rep from * to end. Fasten off.

Tamed Chevron

Multiple of 12 sts (add 2 sts for base chain).

Special abbreviation: dc2tog = work 1dc into next 2 ch or sts indicated leaving 1 loop of each on hook, yo and through all 3 loops on hook.

1st row (wrong side): Skip 3 ch (count as 1dc) and 2dc into next ch, *1dc into each of next 3 ch, dc2tog twice, 1dc into each of next 3 ch, ** [2dc into next ch] twice; rep from * ending last rep at **, 2dc into last ch, turn.

2nd row: 1ch, 1sc into first st, *11ch, skip 11 sts, 1sc into next st; rep from * to end, working last sc into top of tch, turn.

3rd row: 1ch, 1sc into first st, *11sc into 11ch-sp, 1sc into next sc; rep from * to end, turn.

4th row: 1ch, work 1sc into back loop of each st to end, turn.

5th row: 3ch, work 1dc into each st to end. Fasten off.

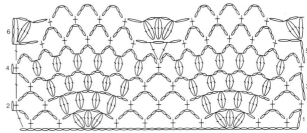

Cavalier Frill

Multiple of 20 sts (add 4 sts for base chain).

Special abbreviations: dc2tog = work 2dc into next st leaving 1 loop of each on hook, yo and through all 3 loops on hook; **bobble** = work 3dc into next st leaving 1 loop of each on hook, yo and through all 4 loops on hook.

1st row (right side): Skip 6 ch (count as 1dc, 3 ch) and 1sc into next ch, 5ch, skip 3 ch, 1sc into next ch, 1ch, skip 3 ch, into next ch work [1 bobble, 1ch] 3 times, *skip 3 ch, 1sc into next ch, [5ch, skip 3 ch, 1sc into next ch] 3 times, 1ch, skip 3 ch, into next ch work [1 bobble, 1ch] 3 times; rep from * to last 9 ch, skip 3 ch, 1sc into next ch, 5ch, skip 3ch, 1sc into next ch, 2ch, 1dc into last ch, turn.

2nd row: 1ch, 1sc into first dc, 5ch, 1sc into first 5ch-arch, 2ch, [1 bobble into next ch sp, 2ch] 4 times, *1sc into next 5ch-arch, [5ch, 1sc into next 5ch-arch] twice, 2ch, [1 bobble into next ch sp, 2ch] 4 times; rep from * to last 2 arches, 1sc into next 5ch-arch, 5ch, skip 2 ch, 1sc into next ch, turn.

3rd row: 5ch (count as 1 dc, 2 ch), 1sc into first 5ch-arch, 3ch, [1 bobble into next ch-sp, 3ch] 5 times, *1sc into next 5ch-arch, 5ch, 1sc into next 5ch arch, 3ch, [1 bobble into next ch-sp, 3ch] 5 times; rep from * to last arch, 1sc into last arch, 2ch, 1dc into last sc, turn.

4th row: 1ch, 1sc into first dc, skip 2-ch sp, *4ch, [1 bobble into next ch-sp, 4ch] 6 times, 1 sc into next 5ch-arch; rep from * to end, placing last sc into 3rd ch of tch, turn.

5th row: 5ch (count as 1dc, 2 ch), skip first 4ch-sp, 1sc into next 4ch-sp, [5ch, 1sc into next 4ch-sp] 4 times, *1ch, into next sc work [1dc, 1ch] twice, skip next 4ch-sp, 1sc into next 4ch-sp, [5ch, 1sc into next 4ch-sp] 4 times; rep from * to last 4ch-sp, 2ch, 1dc into last sc, turn.

6th row: 3ch (count as 1dc), into first dc work (1dc, 1ch, 1 bobble), 1ch, 1sc into next 5ch-arch, [5ch, 1sc into next 5ch-arch] 3 times, *1ch, skip next ch-sp, into next ch-sp work [1 bobble, 1 ch] 3 times, 1 sc into next 5ch-arch, [5ch, 1 sc into next 5ch-arch] 3 times; rep from * to last sp, 1ch, into 3rd ch of tch work (1 bobble, 1ch, dc2tog). Fasten off.

Long-stitch Points

Multiple of 4 sts + 3 sts (add 1 st for base chain).

Special abbreviation: tr2tog 2 rows below = work 1 tr into same st as last tr leaving last loop of tr on hook, skip 3 sts, work 1 tr into next skipped st 2 rows below leaving last loop of tr on hook, yo and through all 3 loops.

Note: work foundation row if working from a base chain.

Foundation row: 1 sc into 2nd ch from hook and each ch to end, turn.

1st row (right side): 1 ch, 1 sc into each of next 3 sts, *1 ch, skip 1 st, 1 sc into each of next 3 sts; rep from * to end, turn.

2nd row: 3 ch (count as 1 dc), skip first sc, work 1 dc into each st to end (working into actual st of each ch, not into ch sp), turn.

3rd row: 1 ch, 1 sc into first dc, 1 tr into first skipped foundation row st, skip 1 dc on 2nd row, 1 sc into next dc, 1 ch, skip 1 dc, 1 sc into next dc, *tr2tog 2 rows below, skip 1 dc on 2nd row, 1 sc into next dc, 1 ch, skip 1 dc, 1 sc into next dc; rep from * to last 2 dc, 1 tr into same ch as 2nd leg of last tr2tog, skip 1 dc, 1 sc into top of tch.
Fasten off.

Chain Swag

Multiple of 8 sts + 1 st (add 1 st for base chain).

Special abbreviation: triple loop = sl st into next sc, [7ch, 1 sl st] 3 times into same sc.

1st row (wrong side): 1 sc into 2nd ch from hook, work 1 sc into each ch to end, turn.

2nd row: 1 ch, work 1 sc into each sc to end, turn.

3rd row: 1 ch, 1 sc into each of first 3 sc, *9ch, skip 3 sc, 1 sc into each of next 5 sc: rep from * to end, omitting 2sc at end of last rep, turn.

4th row: 1 ch, 1 sc into each of first 2sc, *5ch, 1 sc into next 9ch-arch, 5ch, skip 1 sc into each of next 3 sc; rep from * to end, omitting 1 sc at end of last rep, turn.

5th row: 1 ch, 1 sc into first sc, *5ch, skip 1 sc, 1 sc into next sc; rep from * to end, turn.

6th row: 1 ch, 1 sc into first sc, *5ch, work 1 dciple loop into next sc, 5ch, 1 sc into next sc; rep from * to end.
Fasten off

Textured Diamond Edge

Multiple of 6 sts + 1 st (add 1 st for base chain).
Note: work 1st and 2nd rows in color A and 3rd row in color B. Work foundation row if working from a base chain.

Foundation row: 1sc into 2nd ch from hook and each ch to end, turn.

1st row (wrong side): 1ch, sl st into first st, *3ch, skip 2 sts, 1dc into next st, 3ch, skip 2sts, sl st into next st; rep from * to end, turn.

2nd row: 4ch (count as 1dc and 1 ch), 1dc into first sl st, *skip 3ch-sp, sl st into next dc**, skip 3ch-sp, work (1dc, 1ch, 1dc, 1ch, 1dc) into next sl st; rep from * ending last rep at ** in last dc, skip 3ch-sp, work (1dc, 1ch, 1dc) into last sl st, turn.
Fasten off. Join in yarn B.

3rd row: 6ch (count as 1dc and 3 ch), skip (first st, 1ch and 1dc), sl st into next sl st, *3ch, skip 1dc and 1ch, 1dc into next dc, 3ch, skip 1ch and 1dc, sl st into next sl st; rep from * 3ch, skip 1dc and 1ch, 1dc into next ch of tch.
Fasten off.

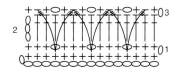

Long-stitch Points

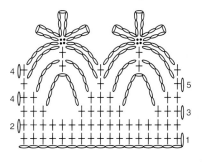

Chain Swag

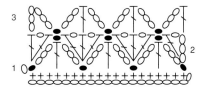

Textured Diamond Edge

2 sc, 1sc into each of next 3 sc, 1ch, into next 4ch-sp work [1dc, 1ch] 6 times, skip 3 sc, 1sc into each of next 3 sc; rep from * to last 2 sc, 1ch, 1hdc into last sc, turn.

5th row: 1ch, 1sc into first hdc, 2ch, [1 bobble into next ch-sp, 2ch] 7 times, *1sc into next 3ch-arch, 2ch, [1 bobble into next ch-sp, 2ch] 7 times; rep from * to last 3 ch, skip 1 ch, 1sc into next ch, turn.

6th row: 1ch, sc into first sc, 2sc into first 2ch-sp, 1sc into top of first bobble, 2sc, into next 2ch-sp, [3ch, 2sc into next sp] twice, 5ch, [2sc into next sp, 3ch] twice, 2sc into next sp, 1sc into top of next bobble, 2sc into next sp, *skip 1 sc, 2sc into next sp, 1sc into top of next bobble, 2sc into next sp, [3ch, 2sc into next sp] twice, 5ch, [2sc into next sp, 3ch] twice, 2sc into next sp, 1 sc into top of next bobble, 2sc into next sp; rep from * to last sc, 1sc into last sc.

Fasten off.

Brontë Fan

Multiple of 17 sts + 2 sts (add 1 st for base chain).

Special abbreviation: bobble = work 3dc into next space leaving 1 loop of each on hook, yo and through all 4 loops on hook.

1st row (right side): 1sc into 2nd ch from hook, work 1sc into each ch to end, turn.

2nd row: 1ch, work 1sc into each sc to end, turn.

3rd row: 1ch, work 1sc into each of first 8 sc, *4ch, skip 3 sc, 1sc into each of next 14 sc; rep from * to last 11 sc, 4ch, skip 3 sc, 1sc into each of last 8 sc, turn.

4th row: 3 ch (count as 1hdc, 1 ch), skip first 2 sc, 1sc into each of next 3 sc, 1ch, into next 4ch-sp work [1dc, 1ch] 6 times, skip 3 sc, 1sc into each of next 3 sc, *3ch, skip

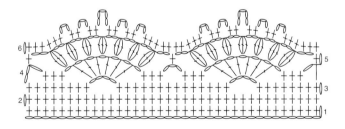

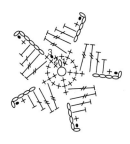

Star Fringe

(1 motif for each repeat).

Note: pattern is worked in a spiral. Do not join at the end of each round.

First motif

Base chain: 2ch.

1st round: 5sc in 2nd ch from hook.

2nd round: 3sc in each sc. (15 sts)

3rd round: [1sc in next st, ch 6, sl st in 2nd ch from hook, 1sc in next ch, 1hdc in next ch, 1dc in next ch, 1tr in next ch, 1tr in bottom of base sc, skip 2 sc] 5 times, sl st in first sc. Fasten off.

Second motif

1st round: 5sc in 2nd ch from hook.

2nd round: 3sc in each sc. (15 sts)

3rd round: [1sc in next st, ch 6, drop loop from hook, insert hook in any point picot of first motif and in dropped loop, draw loop through, sl st in 2nd ch from hook, 1sc in next ch, 1hdc in next ch, 1dc in next ch, 1tr in next ch, 1tr in bottom of base sc, skip 2 sc] 5 times, sl st in first sc.

Fasten off.

Skipping one point to the left of last joining, rep Second motif until required length is reached.

Position along an edge as shown in the photograph and whip stitch to secure.

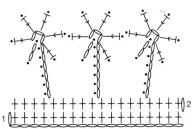

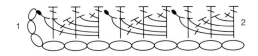

Bullion Stitch Balls

Multiple of 5 sts + 3 sts (add 1 st for base chain).

Special abbreviation: bullion stitch = yo 5 times, insert hook into ch or st indicated, yo, ease the loop through all the loops on hook, 1ch.

1st row (wrong side): 1sc into 2nd ch from hook, work 1sc into each ch to end, turn.

2nd row: 1ch *1sc in each of next 4 sc, 9ch (stem made), sl st into 4th ch from hook (picot made) turn, 2ch (tch) [1 bullion stitch] 5 times into picot, sl st in top of tch, sl st into top of each bullion st, sl st in each ch of stem, 1sc into next sc; rep from * to last 3 sc, 1sc into each of next 3 sc. Fasten off.

Pretty Pockets

Multiple of 3 sts + 1 st (add 2 sts for base chain).

Special abbreviation: pgr (pocket group) = work (1sc, 1hdc, 3dc) around stem of indicated st.

1st row (wrong side): Skip 3 ch (count as 1dc) and 1dc into next ch, work 1dc into each ch to end, turn.

2nd row: 1pgr around first st, skip 2 sts, sl st into top of next st, *1pgr around same st as sl st, skip 2 sts, sl st into top of next st; rep from * to end. Fasten off.

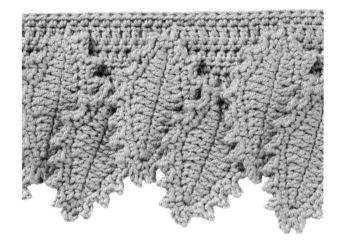

3rd row: 2 ch (count as hdc), skip the st at base of ch, hdc into each st to end, turn.

4th row: 1ch, sc into each st to end, turn.

5th row: 4ch, (count as 1tr), skip the st at base of ch, tr into next 5 sc, *work leaf, 1tr into each of next 6 sc; rep from * to end, turn.

6th row: 2 ch (count as hdc), skip the st at base of ch, hdc into each st to end, turn.

Fasten off.

Leaf Layer

Multiple of 12 sts.

Special abbreviations: picot = 3ch, sl st into first of these ch; **leaf** = 15ch, work in a spiral as follows: sl st into 2nd ch from hook, sl st into each of next 12 ch, 1ch, 1sc into base of ch, working 1 st into each ch, work 1hdc, 3dc, 4tr, 3dc, 1hdc and 1sc, 3ch, then working 1 st into each sl st on other side of base chain, work 1sc, 1hdc, 3dc, 4tr, 3dc, 1hdc, 1sc, 3ch, 1sc into first sc at beg of spiral, 1sc into next hdc, 1 picot, [1sc into each of next 2 sts, 1 picot] 6 times, (1sc, 4ch, sl st into 3rd ch from hook, 1ch, 1sc) into 3ch sp at point of leaf, [1 picot, 1sc into each of next 2 sts] 7 times, sl st into 3ch-sp.

1st row (right side): * Work leaf, 10ch; rep from to * to end.

2nd row: 4 ch (count as 1tr), skip 1 ch and 1tr into next ch 1tr into each st to end, turn.

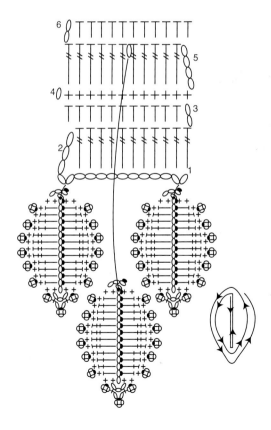

Filet Points

Worked lengthways.

1st row (right side): 5ch, 2dc into 4th ch from hook, 3ch, 3dc into next ch, turn.

2nd row: 5ch (count as 1 dc, 2 ch), skip 3 dc (3dc, 3ch, 3dc) into next 3ch-sp, 2ch, skip 2 dc, 1dc into top of tch, turn.

3rd row: 5ch (count as 1 dc, 2 ch), skip 2ch-sp, 1dc into next dc, 2ch, skip next 2 dc, (3dc, 3ch, 3dc) into next 3ch-sp, turn.

4th row: 5ch (count as 1 dc, 2 ch), skip 3 dc, (3dc, 3ch, 3dc) into next 3ch-sp, 2ch, skip 2 dc, 1dc into next dc, 2ch, skip 2ch-sp, 1dc into next dc, 2ch, skip next 2ch, 1dc into 3rd ch of tch, turn.

5th row: 5ch (count as 1 dc, 2 ch), skip 2ch-sp, 1dc into next dc, [2ch, skip 2ch-sp, 1dc into next dc] twice, 2ch, skip 2 dc, (3dc, 3ch, 3dc) into next 3ch-sp, turn.

6th row: 5ch (count as 1 dc, 2ch), skip 3 dc, (3dc, 3ch, 3dc) into next 3ch-sp, 2ch, skip 2 dc, 1dc into next st, turn.

Rep 3rd to 6th rows until required length is reached, ending with a 5th row.

Fasten off.

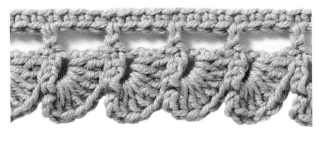

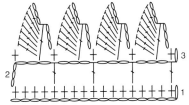

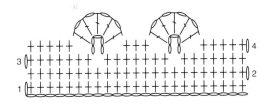

Little Curls

Multiple of 4 sts + 1 st (add 1 st for base chain).

1st row (right side): 1sc into 2nd ch from hook, work 1sc into each ch to end, turn.

2nd row: 6ch (count as 1dc, 3 ch), skip first 4 sc, 1dc into next sc, *3ch, skip 3 sc, 1dc into next sc; rep from * to end.

3rd row: 1 ch, 1sc into first dc, *3ch, 1dc into next sp, 3ch, work 7dc over stem of dc just worked, 1sc into next dc; rep from * to end, placing last sc into 3rd ch of tch. Fasten off.

Large Loop Buttonhole

Multiple of 8 sts + 7 sts (add 1 st for base chain).

Suggestion: work a small sample as described and then adjust the spacing, and the multiple, to suit the project.

1st row (wrong side): 1sc into 2nd ch from hook, work 1sc into each ch to end, turn.

2nd row: 1ch, 1sc into each st to end, turn.

3rd row: 1ch, 1sc into each of first 7 sts, *5ch, skip 1 sc, 1sc into each of next 7 sc; rep from * to end, turn.

4th row: 1ch, 1sc into each of first 5 sts, *skip 2 sc, 1dc into 5ch-sp, [1ch, 1dc] 4 times in same 5ch-sp as last dc, skip 2 sc, 1sc into each of next 3 sc; rep from * to last 2 sts, 1sc in each of next 2 sc. Fasten off.

Portcullis Filet

Worked lengthways over 17 sts (add 3 sts for base chain).

1st row (wrong side): Skip 5 ch (count as 1dc and 1ch-sp) and 1dc into next ch, *1ch, skip 1 ch, 1dc into next ch; rep from * to end, turn.

2nd row: 7ch, 1dc into first dc, [1ch, 1dc into next dc] twice, 7ch, skip 3 dc, [1dc into next dc, 1ch] twice, skip 1ch, 1dc into next ch, turn.

3rd row: 4ch (count as 1dc, 1 ch), skip first dc, 1dc into next dc, 1ch, 1dc into next dc, [1ch, skip 1 ch, 1dc into next ch] 3 times, [1ch, 1dc into next dc] 3 times, turn. Rep 2nd and 3rd rows until required length is reached. Fasten off.

Chain Ruffle

Multiple of any number of sts (add 1 st for base chain).

1st row (right side): 1sc into 2nd ch from hook, work 1sc into each ch to end, turn.

2nd row: 2ch (count as 1 hdc), 1hdc into front loop each sc to end, turn.

3rd row: 1ch, 1sc into back bar under top loops of each hdc to end, turn.

Rep 2nd and 3rd rows then rep 2nd row.

7th row: 1ch, 1 sc into first st, *4ch, 1sc into next sc; rep from * to end, turn.

8th row: 1ch, 1 sc into first st, *6ch, 1sc into next sc; rep from * to end, turn.

9th row: 1ch, 1 sc into first st, *8ch, 1sc into next sc; rep from * to end, turn.

10th row: 1ch, 1 sc into first st, *10ch, 1sc into next sc; rep from * to end, turn.

Fasten off.

Double Chain Arch Edging

Multiple of 3 sts + 2 sts (add 1 st for base chain).

Note: work foundation row if working from a base chain. Scs of 2nd row are always worked immediately to left of scs of 1st row into first of 2 skipped sts of the foundation row or equivalent intervals.

Foundation row: 1sc into 2nd ch from hook and each ch to end, turn.

1st row (right side): Using A, 1ch, 1sc into first st, *5ch, skip 2 sts, 1sc into next st: rep from * to end, ending with 1 st unworked.
Fasten off. Do not turn.

2nd row (right side): Join B at right into 2nd st of foundation row or edge, picking up yarn and drawing through the 5ch-loop of 1st row (so as not to enclose it), work 1sc into same place, *place hook over top of 5ch-loop, yo from behind loop, draw yarn through loop on hook, 4ch, remove hook from working loop, insert hook through next 5ch-loop, pick up working loop again, 1sc into next st; rep from * to end.
Fasten off.

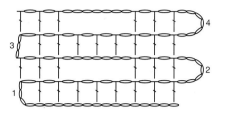

Portcullis Filet

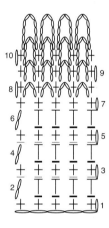

Chain Ruffle

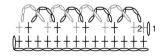

Double Chain Arch Edging

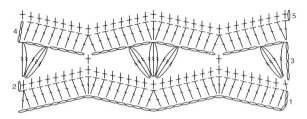

Double Chevron

Multiple of 16 sts + 1 st (add 2 sts for base chain).

Special abbreviations: cluster = work 1dc into same arch as last 3dc leaving 2 loops on hook, skip 1sc, work 1dc into next arch leaving 3 loops on hook, yo and through all 3 loops on hook; **bobble** = work 3tr into next sc leaving 1 loop of each on hook, yo and through all 4 loops on hook.

1st row (right side): Skip 3 ch (count as 1dc) and 1dc into next ch, 1dc into each of next 6 ch, work 3dc into next ch, 1dc into each of next 6 ch, *work 1dc into next ch leaving 2 loops on hook, skip 1 ch, 1dc into next ch leaving 3 loops on hook, yo and through all 3 loops on hook, work 1dc into each of next 6 ch, 3dc into next ch, 1dc into each of next 6 ch; rep from * to last 2 ch, work 1dc into next ch leaving 2 loops on hook, 1dc into last ch leaving 3 loops on hook, yo and through all 3 loops (cluster made at end of row), turn.

2nd row: 1ch, work 1sc into each st to last dc, skip last dc, 1sc into top of tch, turn.

3rd row: 4ch, work 1tr into first sc (half bobble made at beg of row), 2ch, 1 bobble into same sc as half bobble, 4ch, skip 7 sc, 1sc into next sc, *4ch, skip 7 sc, work 1 bobble into next sc, into same sc as last bobble work [2ch, 1 bobble] twice, 4ch, skip 7 sc, 1sc into next sc; rep from * to last 8 sc, 4ch, work 1 bobble into last sc, 2ch, work 2tr into same sc as last bobble leaving 1 loop of each on hook, yo and through all 3 loops on hook (half bobble made at end of row), turn.

4th row: 3ch (count as 1dc), 1dc into top of first half bobble, work 2dc into 2ch-sp, 1dc into next bobble, 3dc into next 4ch-arch, 1 cluster, 3dc into same arch as 2nd leg of last cluster, *1dc into top of next bobble, 2dc into 2ch-sp, 3dc into top of next bobble, 2dc into next 2ch-sp, 1dc into top of next bobble, 3dc into next 4ch-arch, 1 cluster, 3dc into same arch as 2nd leg of last cluster; rep from * to last bobble, 1dc into last bobble, 2dc into next 2ch-sp, 2dc into top of half bobble, turn.

5th row: 1ch, 1sc into each st to end, placing last sc into top of tch.

Fasten off.

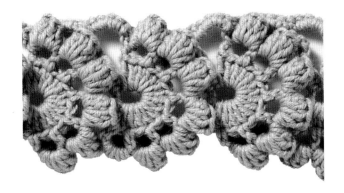

Grand Popcorn Fans

Worked lengthways.

Special abbreviations: popcorn at beg of row = 3ch, work 6dc into first sp, drop loop from hook, insert hook from front into top of 3ch, pick up dropped loop and draw through, 1ch to secure; **7dc-popcorn** = work 7dc into next sp, drop loop from hook, insert hook from front into top of first of these dc, pick up dropped loop and draw through, 1ch to secure.

Make 10ch and join into a ring with a sl st.

1st row (right side): 3ch (count as 1dc), work 14dc into ring, turn.

2nd row: 5ch (count as 1dc, 2 ch), skip first 2 dc, 1dc into next dc, [2ch, skip 1 dc, 1dc into next dc] 6 times placing last dc into 3rd ch of tch, turn.

3rd row: Work 1 popcorn at beg of row, [3ch, 1 7dc-popcorn into next 2ch-sp] 6 times, turn.

4th row: 10ch, skip first 2 ch-sp, work (1sc, 5ch, 1sc) into next 3ch-sp, turn.

5th row: 3ch (count as 1dc), work 14dc into 5ch sp, turn.

Rep 2nd to 5th rows until required length is reached, ending with 3rd row. Do not turn work but continue along side edge as follows:

1st final row: 3ch, 1sc into sp formed at beg of 2nd row of pattern, *5ch, 1sc into sp formed at beg of 4th row of pattern, 5ch, 1sc into sp formed at beg of 2nd row of pattern; rep from * to end, turn.

2nd final row: 1ch, 1sc into first sc, *5sc into 5ch-sp, 1sc into next sc; rep from * to end.

Fasten off.

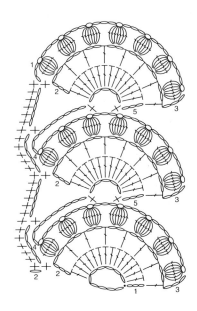

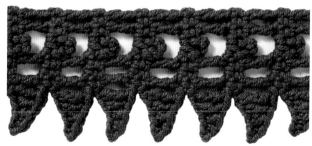

Pintuck Edge

Multiple of any number of sts (add 1 st for base chain).

Using yarn A work a base ch to required length.

1st row (right side): 1sc into 2nd ch from hook, work 1sc into each ch to end, turn.

2nd row: 3ch (count as 1 dc), skip st at base of ch, 1dc into front loop of each sc to end, turn.
Fasten off yarn A. Join in yarn B.

3rd row: 3ch (count as 1 dc) skip st at base of ch, 1dc into back loop of each dc to end, turn.

4th row: 1ch, *insert hook through next dc and corresponding back loop from the st on 2nd row, yo, draw loop through the layers, yo, to complete a sc; rep from * to end.
Fasten off.

Dainty Points

Worked lengthways over 12 sts (add 2 sts for base chain).

1st row (right side): Skip 2 ch, 1sc into next ch, 1hdc into next ch, 1dc into next ch, 1tr into next ch, [1ch, skip 1 ch, 1tr into next ch] twice, 2ch, skip 2 ch, 1tr into each of last 2 ch, turn.

2nd row: 1ch, 1sc into each of first 2 tr, 1sc into 2ch-sp, 4ch, 1sc into same sp as last sc, 1sc into next tr, 1sc into ch-sp, 1sc into next tr, turn.

3rd row: 7ch, work 1sc into 3rd ch from hook, 1hdc into next ch, 1dc into next ch, 1 tr into next ch, 1ch, 1tr into next sc, 1ch, skip 1 sc, 1tr into next sc, 2ch, skip 2 sc, 1tr into each of last 2 sc, turn.
Rep 2nd and 3rd rows until required length is reached.
Fasten off.

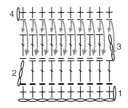

Pintuck Edge

Beaded Dash

Multiple of 2 sts + 1 st (add 1 st for base chain).

Special abbreviation: beaded-dc = yo, insert hook into next st, yo, draw loop through, slide bead along yarn to base of hook, yo, draw yarn through 2 loops, slide bead along yarn to base of hook, yo, draw yarn through remaining 2 loops.

Note: thread beads onto yarn before starting.

1st row (right side): 1sc into 2nd ch from hook, work 1sc into each ch to end, turn.

2nd row: 3ch (count as 1 dc), *1 beaded-dc into next sc, 1dc in next sc; rep from * to end, turn.

3rd row: 1 sl st into front loop of each st to end of row. Fasten off.

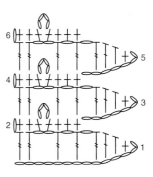

Dainty Points

Beaded Dash

Zigzag Border

Multiple of 6 sts + 1 st (add 1 st for base chain).

Special abbreviations: dtr-grp (double triple group) = work 3dtr into next sc leaving 1 loop of each on hook, yo and through all 4 loops on hook; **double dtr grp** (double triple group) = work 3dtr into same sc as last group leaving 1 loop of each on hook (4 loops on hook), skip 5 sc, into next sc work 3dtr leaving 1 loop of each on hook, yo and through all 7 loops on hook.

1st row (right side): 1sc into 2nd ch from hook, work 1sc into each ch to end, turn.

2nd row: 1ch, work 1sc into each sc to end, turn.

3rd row: 5ch (count as 1dtr), skip first 3 sc, work 1 dtr-grp into next sc, 5ch, *1 double dtr-grp, 5ch; rep from * to last 3 sc, into same sc as last grp work 3dtr leaving 1 loop of each on hook (4 loops on hook), 1dtr into last sc leaving 5 loops on hook, yo and through all 5 loops, turn.

4th row: 1ch, 1sc into top of first grp, 5sc into 5ch-arch, *1sc into top of next grp, 5sc into next 5ch-arch; rep from * to last grp, 1sc into top of tch, turn.

5th row: 1ch, work 1sc into each sc to end.
Fasten off.

Maids in a Row

Multiple of 8 sts + 1 st (add 1 st for base chain).

1st row (right side): 1sc into 2nd ch from hook, work 1sc into each ch to end, turn.

2nd row: 1ch, 1sc into each of first 4 sc, into next sc work (1sc, 7ch, 1sc), *1sc into each of next 7 sc, into next sc work (1sc, 7ch, 1sc); rep from * to last 4 sc, 1sc into each of last 4 sc, turn.

3rd row: 3ch (count as 1dc), skip first sc, *1sc into next sc, 9sc into next arch, skip 3 sc, 1sc into next sc, 1dc into next sc; rep from * to end, turn.

4th row: 1ch, 1sc into first dc, *4ch, skip 5 sc, into next sc work (1sc, 5ch, 1sc), 4ch, skip 5 sc, 1sc into next dc; rep from * to end, placing last sc into top of tch, turn.

5th row: 1ch, 1sc into first sc, *3sc into next 4ch-arch, 5sc into next 5ch-arch, 3sc into next 4ch-arch, 1sc into next sc; rep from * to end.
Fasten off.

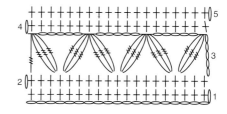

Zigzag Border

Montana Trail

Multiple of 12 sts + 7 sts (add 4 sts for base chain).

Special abbreviation: tr2tog = work 2tr into next st leaving 1 loop of each on hook, yo and through all 3 loops on hook.

1st row (right side): Skip 7 ch, 1dc into next ch, *2ch, skip 2ch, 1dc into next ch; rep from * to end, turn.

2nd row: 1ch, 1sc into first dc, *9ch, skip 1 dc, into next dc work (1sc, 4ch, tr2tog), skip 1dc, into next dc work (tr2tog, 4ch, 1sc); rep from * to last 2 sps, 9ch, skip 1dc, skip next 2 ch, 1sc into next ch, turn.

3rd row: 10ch, 1sc into first 9ch-arch, *4ch, work (tr2tog, 4ch, 1sl st, 4ch, tr2tog) into next tr2tog, 4ch, 1sc into next 9ch-arch; rep from * to end, 4ch, 1ttr into last sc, turn.

4th row: 1ch, 1sc into first ttr, *5ch, skip next 2 4ch-sps, 1sc into next tr2tog; rep from * to end, placing last sc into 6th ch of tch, turn.

5th row: 5ch (count as 1dc, 2 ch), 1dc into next 5ch-arch, 2ch, 1dc into next sc, *2ch, 1dc into next 5ch-arch, 2ch, 1dc into next sc; rep from * to end.

Fasten off.

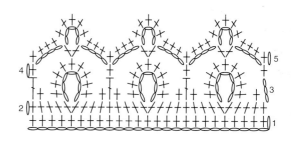

Maids in a Row

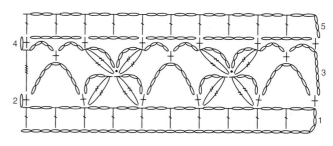

Montana Trail

Lacy Tangle

Multiple of 13 sts + 6 sts (add 3 sts for base chain).

1st row (right side): Skip 3 ch (count as 1dc) and 3dc into next ch, skip 4 ch, 4dc into next ch, *3ch, skip 3 ch, 1sc into next ch, 3ch, skip 3 ch, 4dc into next ch, skip 4 ch, 4dc into next ch; rep from * to end, turn.

2nd row: 3ch (count as 1dc), 3dc into first dc, skip 6 dc, work 4dc into next dc, *3ch, 1sc into next sc, 3ch, 4dc into next dc, skip 6 dc, 4dc into next dc; rep from * to end, placing last group of 4dc into top of 3ch, turn.

3rd row: 6ch (count as 1dc, 3 ch), work 1sc between next 2 groups of 4dc, *3ch, skip 3 dc, 4dc into next dc, skip next 2 3ch-sps, 4dc in next dc, 3ch, 1sc between next 2 groups of 4dc; rep from * to last group, 3ch 1dc into top of tch.

Fasten off.

Chain Buttonhole

Multiple of 8 sts + 5 sts (add 1 st for base chain).

Special abbreviation: picot = 3ch, sl st into 3rd ch from hook.

Suggestion: work a small sample as described and then adjust the spacing, and the multiple, to suit the project.

1st row (right side): 1sc into 2nd ch from hook, work 1sc into each ch to end, turn.

2nd row: 1ch, 1sc into front loop of each st to end, turn.

3rd row: 1ch, 1sc into each of first 5 sts, *7ch, skip 3 sc, 1sc into each of next 5 sc; rep from * to end, turn.

4th row: 1ch, 1sc into each of first 4 sts, *3ch, skip 1 sc and 3 ch, 1sc into next ch, 1 picot, 3ch, skip 3 ch and 1 sc, 1sc into each of next 3 sc; rep from * to last st, 1sc into next sc.

Fasten off.

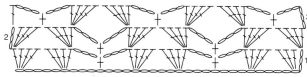

Lacy Triangle

Loopy Edge

Multiple of 2 sts + 1 st (add 1 st for base chain).

Note: for plain loop stitch do not cut loops. The loops are on the back of the fabric as you are working.

Special abbreviation: loop stitch = using the left-hand finger to control loop size, insert hook, pick up both threads of the loop, and draw these through; wrap yarn from the ball over hook and draw through all the loops on hook to complete.

1st row (right side): 1sc into 2nd ch from hook, work 1sc into every ch to end, turn.

2nd row: 1ch, sc into first st, *work loop stitch into next st, sc into next st; rep from * to end, turn.

3rd row: 1ch, 1sc into every st to end, turn.

Rep 2nd and 3rd rows until required depth is reached.

Last row: 1ch, work 1sc into every st to end.

Fasten off.

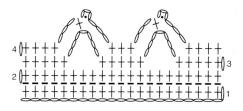

Chain Buttonhole

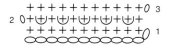

Loopy Edge

Popcorn Wave

Multiple of 10 sts + 1 st (add 1 st for base chain).

Special abbreviation: 5dc-popcorn = work 5dc into indicated st, remove hook from working loop, insert hook under top loops of first of dc sts just worked, hook the working loop and draw this through top loops to draw the popcorn closed, ch1.

Note: work foundation row if working from a base chain.

Foundation row: 1sc into 2nd ch from hook and each ch to end, turn.

1st row (right side): 6ch (counts as 1dc and 3ch), skip 4 sts, 1sc into next st, 1sc into each of next 2 sts, *3ch, skip 3 sts, 5dc-popcorn into next st, 3ch, skip 3 sts, 1sc into each of next 3 sts; rep from * to last 4 sts, 3ch, skip 3 sts, 1dc into last st, turn.

2nd row: 1ch, 1sc into first st, *1sc into next arch, 3ch, skip 1 sc, 5dc-popcorn next sc, 3ch**, 1sc into next arch, 1sc into next 5dc-popcorn; rep from * ending last rep at **, skip 2ch of tch-arch, 1sc into each of next 2ch.
Fasten off.

Cross-topped Fans

Multiple of 4 sts + 1 st (add 1 st for base chain).

Special abbreviation: cross2tr = skip 3 dc, work 1tr into next dc, 2ch, working behind last tr work 1tr into first of skipped dc.

Note: work foundation row if working from a base chain.

Foundation row: 1sc into 2nd ch from hook and each ch to end, turn.

1st row: 3ch (count as 1dc), skip next st, work 4dc into next st, *skip 3 sts, 4dc into next ch; rep from * to last 2 sts, skip 1 st, 1dc into last st, turn.

2nd row: 3ch (count as 1dc), skip st at base of ch, *cross2tr; rep from * to end, 1dc into top of tch, turn.
Fasten off.

Back-and-forth Ruffle

Multiple over any number of sts (add 3 sts for base chain).

1st row: Skip 4 ch (count as 1 tr) and 1tr into next ch or join into an edge and 4ch; work 1tr into each ch or equivalent interval to end, turn.

2nd row: 4ch (count as 1 tr), 1tr into each st to end, do not turn but rotate work 90 degrees so the length worked is facing away and st just worked is at the bottom right. From this point a row is 2 tr running from top of second row to foundation ch.

3rd row: 3ch, *work 6dc around post of first tr, 1dc into base, 6dc around post of next tr in row, 1dc into base of st in next row, 6dc around post of tr just worked into base of, 1dc into top of same tr, 6dc around post of next tr, 1dc into top of st in next row; rep from * to end, omitting last dc in last rep.

Fasten off.

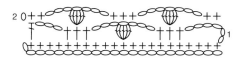

Popcorn Wave

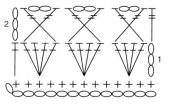

Cross-topped Fans

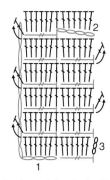

Back-and-forth Ruffle

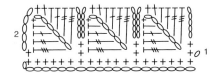

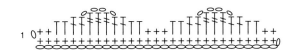

Hanging Blocks

Multiple of 6 sts + 1 st (add 1 st for base chain).

Special abbreviation: wedge picot = work 6ch, 1sc into 2nd ch from hook, 1hdc into next ch, 1dc into next ch, 1tr into next ch, 1dtr into next ch.

Note: work foundation row if working from a base chain.

Foundation row: 1sc into 2nd ch from hook and each ch to end, turn.

1st row (right side): 1ch, 1sc into first st, *1 wedge picot, skip 5 sts, 1sc into next st; rep from * to end, turn.

2nd row: 5ch, *1sc into top of wedge picot, over next 5 ch at underside of wedge picot work 1sc into next ch, 1hdc into next ch, 1dc into next ch, 1tr into next ch, 1dtr into next ch, 5ch, 1sc in next sc**, 5ch; rep from * ending last rep at **.

Fasten off.

Gentle Wave

Multiple of 14 sts + 1 st (add 1 st for base chain).

Note: work foundation row if working from a base chain.

Foundation row: 1sc into 2nd ch from hook work 1sc into each ch to end, turn.

1st row (right side): 1ch, 1sc into first st, or join into an edge, 1ch, 1sc into starting point; counting either sts or equivalent interval, *over next 14 sts, 1sc into next st, [1hdc into next st] twice, [1dc into next st] twice, 1ch, [1tr into next st, 1ch] 3 times, [1dc into next st] twice, [1hdc into next st] twice, [1sc into next st] twice; rep from * to end.

Fasten off.

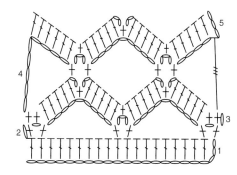

Diamond Edge

Multiple of 9 sts + 2 sts (add 2 sts for base chain).

1st row (right side): Skip 3 ch (count as 1dc) and 1dc into next ch, work 1dc into each ch to end, turn.

2nd row: 1ch, 1sc into first dc, 1ch, 1sc into next dc, 9ch, skip 7 dc, 1sc into next dc, *3ch, 1sc into next dc, 9ch, skip 7 dc, 1sc into next dc; rep from * to end, 1ch, 1sc into top of tch, turn.

3rd row: 1ch, 1sc into first sc, 1sc into first ch-sp, *5dc into next 9ch-arch, 2ch, into same arch as last 5dc work (1sc, 2ch, 5dc), 1sc into next 3ch-arch; rep from * to end, placing last sc into last ch-sp, 1sc into last sc, turn.

4th row: 9ch (count as 1dtr, 4 ch), 1sc into next 2ch-sp, 3ch, 1sc into next 2ch-sp, *9ch, 1sc into next 2ch-sp, 3ch, 1sc into next 2ch-sp; rep from * to last 5dc, 4ch, 1dtr into last sc, turn.

5th row: 3ch (count as 1dc), 5dc into 4ch-arch, 1sc into next 3ch-arch, *5dc into next 9ch-arch, 2ch, into same arch as last 5dc work (1sc, 2ch, 5dc), 1sc into next 3ch-arch; rep from * to last arch, 5dc into last arch, 1dc into 5th ch of tch.

Fasten off.

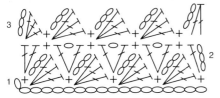

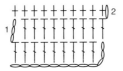

Slanting Shells

Multiple of 4 sts + 1 st (add 1 st for base chain).

Special abbreviation: shell = work (1sc, 3ch, 3dc) in ch or st indicated; **dc2tog** = work 1dc into next 2 ch or sts indicated leaving 1 loop of each on hook, yo and through all 3 loops on hook.

1st row (wrong side): Work 1 shell into 2nd ch from hook, *skip 3 ch, work a shell into next ch; rep from * to last 4 ch, skip 3 ch, 1sc into last ch, turn.

2nd row: 3ch, 1dc into first sc st at base of ch, *skip 3 sts, 1sc into top of 3ch-loop**, work a V st of (1dc, 1ch, 1dc) into next sc; rep from * ending last rep at **, 2dc into last sc, skip tch, turn.

3rd row: 3ch, 3dc into first st, skip next st, *work a shell into next sc, skip next V st; rep from * ending 1sc into last sc, 3ch, dc2tog over last dc and top of tch.

Fasten off.

Unpicked Fringe

Multiple of any number of sts (add 2 sts for base chain).

Note: This edging does unravel with age and hard wear. For extra strength, work a row of running stitch along the top of the posts of the dc of the first row.

Using waste yarn work a base ch to required length.

Foundation row: Skip 3 ch, (count as 1 dc) 1dc into each ch to end, turn.

Join in working yarn.

1st row: 3ch (count as 1 dc) 1dc into each st to end, turn.

2nd row: 1ch, 1sc into each st to end.

Cut the waste yarn through the posts of each dc and remove it.

Fasten off.

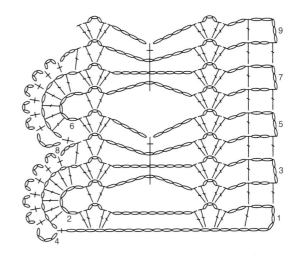

Light Shell Frill

Worked lengthways.

1st row (wrong side): 26ch, 1dc into 8th ch from hook, 2ch, skip 2 ch, 2dc into next ch, 3ch, 2dc into next ch, 9ch, skip 10 ch, 2dc into next ch, 3ch, 2dc into next ch, leaving 2 ch unworked, turn.

2nd row: 6ch, skip 2 dc, (1dc, 3ch, 1dc) into next 3ch-sp, 9ch, skip 9ch-sp and 2 dc, (2dc, 3ch, 2dc) into next 3ch-sp, 2ch, skip 2 dc and ch-sp, 1dc into next st, 2ch, skip 2ch, 1dc into next ch of tch, turn.

3rd row: 5ch (count as 1dc, 2ch), skip 1 dc at base of ch, 1dc into next dc, 2ch, skip 2ch-sp and 2 dc, (2dc, 3ch, 2dc) into next 3ch-sp, 9ch, skip 2 dc and 9ch-sp, (2dc, 3ch, 2dc) into next 3ch-sp, [1ch, 1dc] 7 times into 6ch-sp, 1ch, 1sc

into last ch of foundation ch or in foll repeats into last dc of last fan motif, turn.

4th row: 4ch, skip 1ch-sp, [1sc into next 1ch-sp, 3ch] 6 times, 1dc into next 1ch-sp, (1dc, 3ch, 1dc) into next 3ch-sp, 9ch, skip 2 dc and 9ch-sp, (2dc, 3ch, 2dc) into next 3ch-sp, 2ch, skip 2 dc, and 2ch-sp, 1dc into next st, 2ch, 1dc into 3rd ch of tch, turn.

5th row: 5ch (count as 1dc, 2ch), skip 1 dc at base of ch, 1dc into next dc, 2ch, skip 2ch-sp and 2 dc, (2dc, 3ch, 2dc) into next 3ch-sp, 4ch, 1sc around last 3 9ch-strands, 4ch, skip next dc, (2dc, 3ch, 2dc) into next 3ch-sp, turn.

Rep 2nd to 5th rows until required length is reached.
Fasten off.

Floral Trellis

Worked lengthways over 28 sts (add 3 sts for base chain).

1st row (right side): Skip 6 ch, work 1dc into next ch from hook, [2ch, skip 2 ch, 1dc into next ch] 8 times, turn. (9 sps)

2nd row: 5ch (count as 1dc, 2 ch), skip first dc, 1dc into next dc, [2ch, 1dc into next dc] 3 times, 5ch, skip next 4 sps, 1dc into next sp, work [3ch, 1dc] 3 times into same sp as last dc, turn.

3rd row: 1ch, 1sc into first dc, into first 3ch-sp work (1hdc, 1dc, 1tr, 1dc, 1hdc, 1sc), into next 3ch-sp work (1sc, 1hdc, 1dc, 1tr, 1dc, 1hdc, 1sc), into next 3ch-sp work (1sc, 1hdc, 1dc, 1tr, 1dc, 1hdc), 1sc into next dc, 5ch, 1dc into next dc, [2ch, 1dc into next dc] 4 times placing last dc into 3rd ch of tch, turn.

4th row: 5ch (count as 1dc, 2 ch), skip first dc, [1dc into next dc, 2ch] 4 times, 1dc into 5ch-sp, 7ch, skip first group of 7 sts, work 1dc into tr at center of next group of 7 sts, [3ch, 1dc] 3 times into same st as last dc, turn.

5th row: 1ch, 1sc into first dc, into first 3ch-sp work (1hdc, 1dc, 1tr, 1dc, 1hdc, 1sc), into next 3ch-sp work (1sc, 1hdc, 1dc, 1tr, 1dc, 1hdc, 1sc), into next 3ch-sp work (1sc, 1hdc, 1dc, 1tr, 1dc, 1hdc), 1sc into next dc, 5ch, 1dc into 7ch-sp, [2ch, 1dc into next dc] 6 times placing last dc into 3rd ch of tch, turn.

6th row: 5ch (count as 1dc, 2 ch), skip first dc, [1dc into next dc, 2ch] 6 times, 1dc into 5ch-sp, 7ch, skip first group of 7 sts, work 1dc into tr at center of next group of 7 sts, [3ch, 1dc] 3 times into same st as last dc, turn.

7th row: 1ch, 1sc into first dc, into first 3ch-sp work (1hdc, 1dc, 1tr, 1dc, 1hdc, 1sc), into next 3ch-sp work (1sc, 1hdc, 1dc, 1tr, 1dc, 1hdc, 1sc), into next 3ch-sp work (1sc, 1hdc, 1dc, 1tr, 1dc, 1hdc), 1sc into next dc, 5ch, 1dc into 7ch-sp, [2ch, 1dc into next dc] 8 times placing last dc into 3rd ch of tch, turn.

Rep 2nd to 7th rows until required length is reached, ending with a 7th row.

Fasten off.

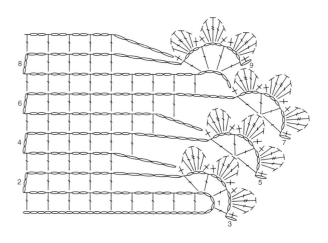

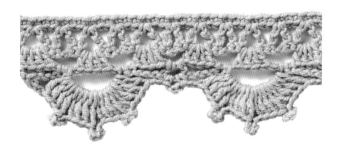

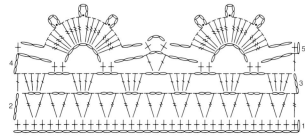

Fan Flair

Multiple of 18 sts + 17 sts (add 1 st for base chain).

1st row (right side): 1sc into 2nd ch from hook, work 1sc into each ch to end, turn.

2nd row: 4ch (count as 1tr), *skip next 2 sc, work (1tr, 2ch, 1tr) into next sc; rep from * to last 2 sc, 1tr into last sc, turn.

3rd row: 3ch (count as 1dc), work 4dc into first 2ch-sp, *3ch, skip 2ch-sp, 4dc into next 2ch-sp; rep from * to end, 1dc into 4th ch of tch, turn.

4th row: 6ch (count as 1dc, 3 ch), 2sc into first 3ch-sp, 7ch, 2sc into next 3ch-sp, *3ch, into next 3ch-sp work (1dc, 2ch, 1dc), 3ch, 2sc into next 3ch-sp, 7ch, 2sc into next 3 ch-sp; rep from * to last 5 sts, 3ch, 1dc into 3rd ch of tch, turn.

5th row: 1ch, 1sc into first dc, 2ch, into 7ch-arch work 4tr and [5ch, sl st into first of these ch, 4tr] 3 times, 2ch, *skip 3ch-sp, into next 2ch-sp work (1sc, 3ch, 1sc), 2ch, into 7ch-arch work 4tr and [5ch, sl st into first of these ch, 4tr] 3 times; rep from * to last sp, 2ch, 1sc into 3rd ch of tch. Fasten off.

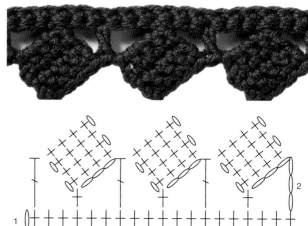

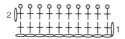

Simple Beaded Edge

Any number of sts (add 1 st for base chain).

Special abbreviation: pb (place bead) = slide next bead along yarn to base of hook.

Note: thread beads onto yarn before starting.

1st row (right side): 1sc into 2nd ch from hook work 1sc into each ch to end, turn.

2nd row: 1ch, pb, 1sc into first sc, *pb, 1sc in next sc; rep from * to end.

Fasten off.

Flying Diamonds

Multiple of 6 sts + 1 st (add 1 st for base chain).

Note: work foundation row if working from a base chain.

Foundation row: 1sc into 2nd ch from hook and each ch to end, turn.

1st row (right side): 6ch (counts as 1dc and 3ch), skip first 3 sts, 1sc into next st, (1dc and 3ch sp formed at beg of row), turn, 1ch, 1sc into sc just worked, 3sc into 3ch-sp, [turn, 1ch 1sc into each of the 4 sc] 3 times, skip next 2 sts on foundation row, 1dc into next st, *3ch, miss next 2 sts on foundation row, 1sc into next st, turn, 1ch, 1sc into sc just worked, 3sc into 3ch-sp, [turn, 1ch, 1sc into each of the 4 sc] 3 times, skip next 2 sts on foundation row, 1dc, into next st; rep from * to end.

Fasten off.

Triangle Edge

Multiple of 19 sts (1 motif for each repeat).

Motif

Base ring: 6ch, join with sl st to form a ring.

1st round: 4ch (count as 1 dc, 1 ch), 1dc into ring, *[2ch, 1dc, 1ch, 1dc] 5 times, 2ch, sl st to 3rd ch of tch.

2nd round: 1ch, *1sc into next sp, [1dc, 1ch] twice into next sp, 1dc into same sp; rep from * 5 more times, sl st to first sc.

3rd round: 3ch (count as 1 sc, 1 ch), *[1sc into next 1ch-sp, 1ch] twice, (1tr, 1ch, 1dtr, 5ch, 1dtr, 1ch, 1tr) into next sc for a corner group, [1ch, 1sc into next 1ch-sp] twice, 1ch**, 1sc into next sc, 1ch; rep from * once more, then from * to ** again, sl st to 3rd ch of tch.

Fasten off.

Header

With WS facing and using the diagram as a guide, rejoin yarn in corner 5ch-sp to the far right of the first motif.

1st row: 3ch (count as 1 dc), 1dc into the corner-sp, 1dc into next 2 sts [1dc into next 1ch-sp, 1dc into next st] 5 times, 1dc into next 1ch-sp, 1dc into next 2 sts, 2dc into the corner-sp, *2dc into the corner-sp of next motif, 1dc into next 2 sts, [1dc into next 1ch-sp, 1dc into next st] 5 times, 1dc into next 1ch-sp, 1dc into next 2 sts, 2dc into the corner-sp; rep from * across each motif to end.

2nd row: 2ch, work 1hdc into each st to end, turn.

3rd row: 1ch, 1sc into back loop of each st to end, turn.

4th, 5th and 6th rows: 1ch, 1sc into each st to end, turn.

Fasten off.

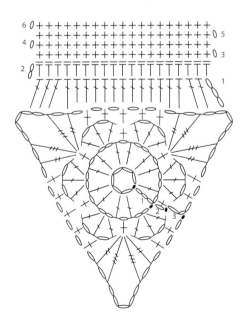

Two-row Bobbles

Multiple of 6 sts + 1 st (add 4 sts for base chain).

Special abbreviations: dc2tog = work to 2dc into next st leaving 1 loop of each on hook, yo and through all 3 loops on hook; **shell** = work (dc2tog, 1dc, dc2tog) all into next st; **group** = into first dc2tog of shell work 2dc leaving 1 loop of each on hook (3 loops on hook), 1dc into dc of same shell leaving 4 loops on hook, into 2nd dc2tog of shell work 2dc leaving 1 loop of each on hook, yo and through all 6 loops.

1st row (right side): Skip 7 ch (1dc and 2 ch sp at beg of row) and 1dc into next ch or join into an edge and 5ch, skip 2 st equivalent sp, 1dc in next st equivalent sp; counting either ch or equivalent interval, *1ch, skip 2 ch, work 1 shell into next ch, 1ch, skip 2 ch, 1dc into next ch; rep from * to last 3 ch, 2ch, skip 2 ch, 1dc into last ch, turn.

2nd row: 5ch (count as 1dc, 2 ch), skip first dc, 1dc into next dc, 2ch, *work 1 group over next shell, 2ch, 1dc into next dc, 2ch; rep from * to last dc, skip 2 ch, 1dc into next ch. Fasten off.

Honeycomb Edge

Multiple of 5 sts + 1 st (add 1 st for base chain).

1st row (right side): 1sc into 2nd ch from hook, work 1sc into each ch to end, turn.

2nd row: 1ch, 1sc into each of first 2 sc, *5ch, skip 2 sc, 1sc into each of next 3 sc; rep from * to end, omitting 1sc at end of last rep, turn.

3rd row: 1ch, 1sc into first sc, *5sc into next 5ch-arch, skip 1 sc, 1sc into next sc; rep from * to end, turn.

4th row: 6ch (count as 1tr, 2 ch), skip first 2 sc, 1sc into each of next 3 sc, *5ch, skip 3 sc, 1sc into each of next 3 sc; rep from * to last 2 sc, 2ch, 1tr into last sc, turn.

5th row: 1ch, 1sc into first tr, 2sc into 2ch-sp, skip 1 sc, 1sc into next sc, *skip 1 sc, 5sc into next 5ch-arch, skip 1 sc, 1sc into next sc; rep from * to last 2ch-sp, 2sc into last sp, 1sc into 4th ch of tch. Fasten off.

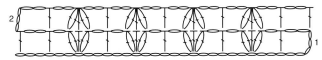

Two-row Bobbles

Single Rib

Multiple of 2 sts (add 2 sts for base chain).

Special abbreviations: dc/rf (raised double crochet at the front of the fabric) = yo, insert hook from in front and from right to left around the stem of the appropriate stitch, and complete stitch normally; **dc/rb** (raised double crochet at the back of the fabric) = yo, insert hook from behind and from right to left around the stem of the appropriate stitch, and complete stitch normally.

1st row (wrong side): Skip 3 ch (count as 1dc) and 1dc into next ch or join into an edge and 3ch; work 1dc into each ch or equivalent interval to end, turn.

2nd row: 2ch (count as 1dc), skip first st at base of ch, *1dc/rf around next st, 1dc/rb around next st; rep from * ending 1dc into top of tch, turn.

Rep 2nd row until required depth is reached.

Fasten off.

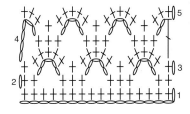

Honeycomb Edge

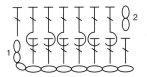

Single Rib

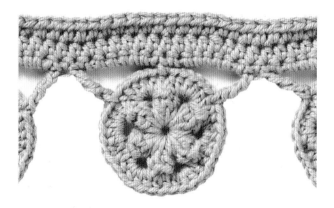

Medallion Dangle

Multiple of 14 sts (1 motif for each repeat).

Special abbreviation: 4dc-popcorn = work 4dc into indicated st, remove hook from working loop, insert hook under top loops of first of dc sts just worked, hook the working loop and draw this through top loops to draw the popcorn closed, ch1.

Motif

Base ring: 7ch, join with sl st.

1st round: 3ch, 3dc into ring, remove hook and insert through top of tch and into loop and draw through loop on hook (popcorn made), 3ch, [4dc-popcorn into ring, 3ch] 5 times, sl st to top of first popcorn.

2nd round: 2ch, (count as 1hdc) 1hdc into same place as sl st, *4hdc into next 3ch-sp, 2hdc into top of next popcorn; rep from *4 more times, 4hdc into 3ch-sp, sl st to top of 3ch. Fasten off.

Header

Rejoin yarn with a sl st between any 2hdc on the first motif.

1st row: 11ch (count as 1 dtr, 6 ch), *skip next 6 hdc, 1sc between next 2hdc of motif, 6ch, skip next 6 hdc, 1dtr between next 2hdc of motif, 1dtr between any 2hdc of next medallion, 6ch; rep from * to the last motif, skip next 6 hdc, 1sc between next 2hdc of motif, 6ch, skip next 6 hdc, 1dtr between next 2hdc of motif, turn.

2nd row: 1ch, 1sc into tr, 6sc into 6ch-sp, *1sc into next sc, 6sc into 6ch-sp, 1sc in each of next 2 dtr, 6sc in next 6ch-sp; rep from * to last sc, 1sc into next sc, 6sc into 11ch-sp, 1sc into 4ch of tch, turn.

3rd and 4th rows: 2ch, work 1hdc into each st to end, turn. Fasten off.

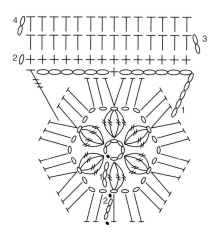

Chain Walk

Multiple of 8 sts + 1 st (add 1 st for base chain).

Special abbreviation: bobble = work 4dc into next st leaving 1 loop of each on hook, yo and through all 5 loops on hook.

1st row (wrong side): 1sc into 2nd ch from hook, work 1sc into each ch to end, turn.

2nd row: 4ch (count as 1dc, 1ch), skip first 2sc, 1 bobble into next sc, 1ch, skip 1 sc, 1dc into next sc, *1ch, skip 1 sc, 1 bobble into next sc, 1ch, skip 1 sc, 1dc into next sc; rep from * to end, turn.

3rd row: 1ch, work 1sc into each dc, ch-sp and bobble to end, working last 2 sc into 4th and 3rd ch of tch, turn.

4th row: 1ch, 1sc into each of first 3 sc, *5ch, skip 3 sc, 1sc into each of next 5 sc; rep from * to end, omitting 2sc at end of last rep, turn.

5th row: 1ch, 1sc into each of first 2 sc, *3ch, 1sc into 5ch-arch, 3ch, skip 1 sc, 1sc into each of next 3 sc; rep from * to end, omitting 1sc at end of last rep, turn.

6th row: 1ch, 1sc into first sc, *3ch, 1sc into next 3ch-arch, 1sc into next sc, 1sc into next 3ch-arch, 3ch, skip 1 sc, 1sc into next sc; rep from * to end, turn.

7th row: 5ch (count as 1dc, 2 ch), 1sc into next 3ch-arch, 1sc into each of next 3 sc, 1sc into next 3ch-arch, *5ch, 1sc into next 3ch-arch, 1sc into each of next 3 sc, 1sc into next 3ch-arch; rep from * to last sc, 2ch, 1dc into last sc, turn.

8th row: 1ch, 1sc into first dc, *3ch, skip 1 sc, 1sc into each of next 3 sc, 3ch, 1sc into next 5ch-arch; rep from * to end, placing last sc into 3rd ch of tch, turn.

9th row: 1ch, 1sc into first sc, *1sc into next 3ch-arch, 3ch, skip 1 sc, 1sc into next sc, 3ch, 1sc into next 3ch-arch, 1sc into next sc; rep from * to end.
Fasten off.

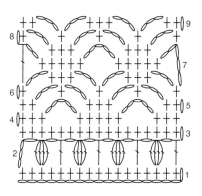

Arrowhead Fans

Multiple of 10 sts + 1 st (add 2 sts for base chain).

1st row (right side): Skip 3 ch (count as 1dc) and 1dc into next ch, work 1dc into each ch to end, turn.

2nd row: 1ch, 1sc into each of first 3 dc, *2ch, skip 2 dc, into next dc work [2dc, 2ch] twice, skip 2 dc, 1sc into each of next 5 dc; rep from end, omitting 2sc at end of last rep and placing last sc into top of tch, turn.

3rd row: 1ch, 1sc into each of first 2 sc, *3ch, skip next 2ch-sp, into next 2ch-sp work (3dc, 2ch, 3dc), 3ch, skip 1 sc, 1sc into each of next 3 sc; rep from * to end, omitting 1sc at end of last rep, turn.

4th row: 1ch, 1sc into first sc, *4ch, skip next 3ch-sp, into next 2ch-sp work (4dc, 2ch, 4dc), 4ch, skip 1 sc, 1sc into next sc; rep from * to end, turn.

5th row: 1ch, 1sc into first sc, *5ch, skip next 4ch-sp, into next 2ch-sp work (4dc, 2ch, 4dc), 5ch, 1sc into next sc; rep from * to end.

Fasten off.

Double Loops

Multiple of 3 sts (add 1 st for base chain).

1st row (right side): 1sc into 2nd ch from hook, 1sc into back bump of each ch to end, turn.

2nd row: 1ch, 1sc into each of first 3 sc, *4ch, 1sc into each of next 3 sc; rep from * to end, turn.

3rd row: 1ch, 1sc in each of first 2 sts, *skip 1 sc, 1dc in 4ch-sp, [3ch, sl st in 3rd ch from hook, 1dc in 4ch-sp] 4 times, skip 1 sc, 1sc into next sc; rep from * to last sc, 1sc in last sc.

Fasten off. Do not turn work.

With edge just worked hanging downwards, rejoin yarn under far right ch loop of foundation ch.

Rep 1st to 3rd rows along this edge.

Fasten off.

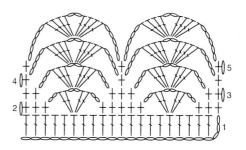

Arrowhead Fans

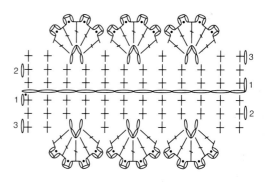

Double Loops

Curlicue

Worked lengthways over 8 sts (add 2 sts for base chain).

1st row (wrong side): 9ch, 1hdc into 3rd ch from hook, *1ch, skip 1 ch1, hdc into next ch; rep from * to end, turn.

2nd row: 2ch, 1hdc into first ch-sp, *1ch, 1hdc into next ch-sp; rep from to end, turn.

Rep 2nd row.

4th row: 2ch, 1hdc into first ch-sp, *1ch, 1hdc into next ch-sp; rep from to end, 20ch, turn.

5th row: 3dc into 4th ch from hook, 3sc into back bump of next 15 ch, (1dc, 1hdc, 1sc) into next ch, *1ch, 1hdc into next ch-sp; rep from * to end.

Rep 2nd to 5th rows until required length is reached. Fasten off.

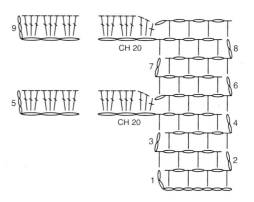

Curlicue

Flower Trail

Worked lengthways.

Note: on 2nd row check that each Base Flower Unit is not twisted before you work into it.

1st row (right side): 7ch, *sl st into 4th ch from hook, 3ch, into ring just formed work a Base Flower Unit of (2dc, 3ch, sl st, 3ch, 2dc)**, 10ch; rep from * ending last rep at ** when edging is required length, then keep same side facing and rotate so as to be able to work along underside of Base Flower Units.

2nd row (right side): *3ch, sl st into ch ring at center of Flower, 3ch, (2dc, 3ch, sl st, 3ch, 2dc) all into same ring, skip 2ch of base chain that connects Units, sl st into next ch**, 2ch, skip 2ch, sl st into next ch; rep from * into next and each Base Flower Unit to end, ending at **.
Fasten off.

Roundel Run

(1 motif for each repeat).

Buckle motif

1st round: 18ch, sl st to first ch, turn and 7ch, sl st to opposite side of circle.

2nd round: Sl st into next ch, 1sc into each of 18 ch around, sl st to first sc.
Fasten off.
Rep Buckle Motif until required length is reached.

Linking motif

1st round: 18ch, thread the ch under the cross bar of two Buckle Motifs, join with sl st.

2nd round: 1ch, 1sc into each ch around, sl st to first sc.
Fasten off.
Rep Linking Motif until all Buckle Motifs are joined.
Using some of the ends, whip stitch to secure to edge.

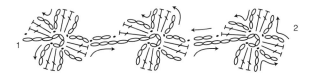

Flower Trail

Snowdrop Picots

Worked lengthways.

Make 4ch (count as 1dc, 1ch).

1st row (wrong side): Work 2dc into first of these ch, 2ch, 3dc into same ch as last 2 dc, turn.

2nd row: 8ch, sl st into 6th ch from hook, 7ch, sl st into same ch as last sl st, 5ch, sl st into same ch as last 2 sl sts, 2ch, 3dc into 2ch-sp of next shell, 2ch, 3dc into same sp as last 3dc, turn.

3rd row: Sl st into each of first 3dc, 3ch (count as 1dc), 2dc into 2ch-sp, 2ch 3dc into same sp as last 2dc, turn.

Rep 2nd and 3rd rows until required length is reached, ending with a 2nd row. Do not turn work but continue along side edge as follows:

Final row: *3ch, 1sc into top of tch beg of next fan, 3ch, 1sc into first sl st at beg of next fan; rep from * to last fan, 1sc into top of tch of 1st row.

Fasten off.

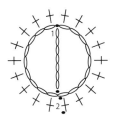

Roundel Run

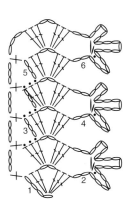

Snowdrop Picots

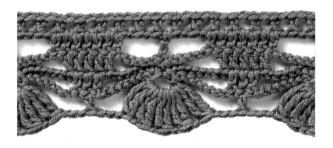
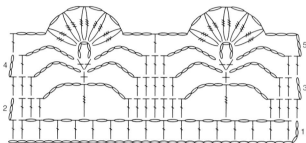

Fan Parade

Multiple of 16 sts + 1 st (add 2 sts for base chain).
Special abbreviation: cluster = work 2dtr into next st leaving 1 loop of each on hook, yo and through all 3 loops on hook.

1st row (right side): Skip 3 ch (count as 1dc) and 1dc into next ch, *1ch, skip 1 ch, 1dc into next ch; rep from * to last ch, 1dc into last ch, turn.

2nd row: 3ch (count as 1dc), skip first dc, 1dc into each of next dc, ch-sp and dc, 5ch, skip 2 sps, 1tr into next sp, 5ch, skip 2 dc, 1dc into next dc, *[1dc into next sp, 1dc into next dc] 3 times, 5ch, skip 2 sps, 1tr into next sp, 5ch, skip 2 dc, 1dc into next dc; rep from * to last 3 sts, 1dc into next sp, 1dc into next dc, 1dc into top of tch, turn.

3rd row: 3ch, skip first dc, 1dc into each of next 2 dc, 7ch, 1sc into next tr, 7ch, *skip 1 dc, 1dc into each of next 5 dc, 7ch, 1sc into next tr, 7ch; rep from * to last 4 sts, skip 1 dc, 1dc into each of next 2 dc, 1dc into top of tch, turn.

4th row: 3ch, skip first dc, 1dc into next dc, 7ch, into next sc work (1sc, 5ch, 1sc), 7ch, *skip 1 dc, 1dc into each of next 3 dc, 7ch, into next sc work (1sc, 5ch, 1sc), 7ch; rep from * to last 3 sts, skip 1 dc, 1dc into next dc, 1dc into top of tch, turn.

5th row: 6ch (count as 1dc, 3 ch), *skip 7ch-arch, work 1 cluster into 5ch-arch then [1ch, 1 cluster] 4 times into same arch, 3ch, skip 1 dc, 1dc into next dc, 3ch; rep from * to end, omitting 3ch at end of last rep and placing last dc into top of tch.
Fasten off.

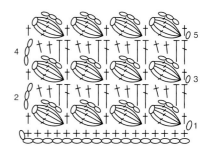

Popcorn Cobbles

Multiple of 4 sts + 1 st (add 1 st for base chain).

Special abbreviation: 5dc-popcorn = work 5dc into indicated st, remove hook from working loop, insert hook under top loops of first of the dc sts just worked, hook the working loop and draw this through top loops to draw the popcorn closed, ch1.

Note: work foundation row if working from a base chain.

Foundation row: 1sc into 2nd ch from hook and each ch to end, turn.

1st row (right side): 1ch, 1sc into first st, *3ch, 5dc-popcorn into same place as sc, skip 3 sts, 1sc into next st; rep from * to end, turn.

2nd row: 3ch (count as 1dc), skip first st, *1sc into each of next 2 ch, 1hdc into next ch, 1dc into next sc; rep from * to end, skip tch, turn.

3rd row: 1ch, 1sc into first st, *3ch, 5dc-popcorn into same place as sc, skip next 3 sts, 1sc into next dc; rep from * ending last rep in top of tch, turn.

Rep 2nd and 3rd rows once more.

Fasten off.

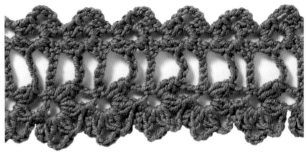

Six-point Snowflake

Multiple of 3 sts + 2 sts (add 1 st for base chain).

Special abbreviation: picot = 4ch, sl st into 4th ch from hook.

1st row (right side): Skip 2 ch (count as 1 hdc), 1hdc into next ch, 1hdc into each ch to end, turn.

2nd row: 2ch (count as 1 hdc), *1hdc into next hdc, 1 picot, 8ch, sl st into 8th ch from hook, 10ch, sl st into 10th ch from hook, 14ch, sl st into 14th ch from hook, 3 picots, 4ch, (for the following picots, work on the other side of the picots just made and sl st into base ch of respective picot of the other side after completing each one), 3 picots, 14ch, sl st into 14th ch from hook, 10ch, sl st into 10th ch from hook, 8ch, sl st into 8th ch from hook, 1 picot, sl st on top of hdc just made, 1hdc into each of next 2 sts; rep from * to end.

Fasten off.

Highland Edge

Worked lengthways.

Special abbreviations: 2dc-cluster = work 2dc into next space leaving 1 loop of each on hook, yo and draw through all 3 loops on hook; **3dc-cluster** = work 3dc into next space leaving 1 loop of each on hook, yo and draw through all 4 loops on hook.

1st row (right side): 12ch, 2dc into 6th ch from hook, 3ch, 2dc into same ch as last 2dc, 5ch, skip 5 ch, 1sc into next ch, 5ch, 1sc into same ch as last sc, turn.

2nd row: 4ch, work 2dc-cluster into first 5ch-sp, work [5ch, 1 3dc-cluster] 3 times into same 5ch-sp, 5ch, skip next 5ch-sp, skip 2 dc, work into 3ch-sp (2dc, 3ch, 2dc) turn.

3rd row: 5ch, skip 2 dc, work into the 3ch-sp (2dc, 3ch, 2dc), 5ch, skip next 5ch-sp, 1sc into next 5ch-sp, 5ch, 1sc into same ch-sp as last sc, turn.

Rep 2nd and 3rd rows until required length is reached, ending with a 2nd row.

Fasten off.

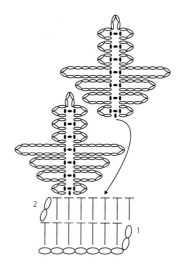

Six-point Snowflake

Leaf Filet

Worked lengthways over 19 sts (add 4 sts for base chain).

Special abbreviations: open mesh = 1ch, skip 1 ch or dc, 1dc into next dc st; **solid mesh** = 1dc into next ch-sp or st, 1dc into next dc st.

Note: read the chart from right to left on odd numbered rows and left to right on even numbered rows.

1st row (right side as chart): Skip 6 ch, 1dc into next ch (first mesh completed), cont to end of row using chart as reference and counting each ch as either a sp or a st, turn.

2nd row: 3ch (counts as 1 dc), cont to end of row, work last dc into top of tch, turn.

Cont to foll the chart, 3ch (counts as 1 dc) at beg of each row, and work last dc into into top of tch before turning.

Rep 2nd to 7th chart rows until required length is reached. Fasten off.

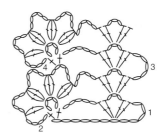

Highland Edge

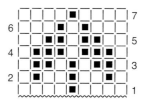

Leaf Filet

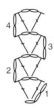

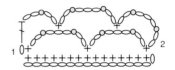

Rickrack

Worked lengthways.

Special abbreviation: shell = work (1sc, 2ch, 1sc) into next space indicated.

1st row (right side): *3ch, 1 shell into 3rd ch from hook, turn.

2nd row: 2ch, 1 shell into 2ch-sp of previous shell, turn.

Rep 2nd row until required length is reached.

Fasten off.

Beaded Diamond Picot

Multiple of 7 sts + 1 st (add 1 st for base chain).

Special abbreviation: pb (place bead) = slide next bead along yarn to base of hook.

Note: work foundation row if working from a base chain. Thread beads onto yarn before starting.

Foundation row: 1sc into 2nd ch from hook and each ch to end, turn.

1st row (wrong side): 1ch, 1sc into first st, *2ch, pb, 3ch, pb, 2ch, skip 6 sts, 1sc in next st; rep from * to end, turn.

2nd row: 2ch, pb, 3ch, pb, 2ch, 1sc in ch-sp between beads of previous row, *2ch, pb, 3ch, pb, 2ch, 1sc in ch-sp; rep from * to last 3ch-sp, 2ch, pb, 2ch, dc in sc.

Rep 2nd row until required depth is reached.

Fasten off.

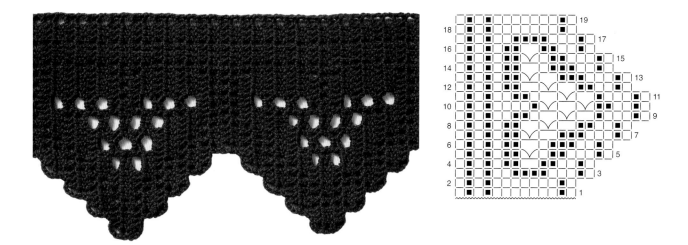

Heart Filet

Worked lengthways over 27 sts (add 4 sts for base chain).
Special abbreviations: open mesh = 1ch, skip 1 ch or dc, 1dc into next dc st; **solid mesh** = 1dc into next ch-sp or st, 1dc into next dc st; **lacet** (worked over 2 mesh blocks) = **1st row:** 2ch, skip 1 ch or dc, 1sc into next ch or st, 2ch, skip 1 ch or dc, 1dc into next dc st. **2nd row:** 3ch, skip next 2 2ch-sp, 1dc into next dc st.
Note: read the chart from right to left on odd numbered rows and left to right on even numbered rows.

1st row (right side as chart): Skip 6 ch, 1dc into next ch (first mesh completed), cont to end of row using the chart as reference and counting each ch as either a sp or a st, turn.

2nd row: 3ch (counts as 1 dc), cont to end of row, work last dc into top of tch, turn.

3rd row (increase row): 8ch, skip 6 ch, 1dc into next ch (first mesh completed), cont to end of row, turn.
Cont to foll the chart, 3ch (counts as 1 dc) at the beg of row, start increase rows as the 3rd row and work last dc into into top of tch before turning.
Rep 2nd to 19th rows until required length is reached. Fasten off.

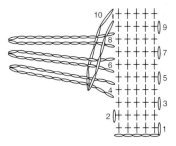

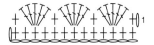

Bunched Fringe

Worked lengthways over 5 sts (add 1 st for base chain).

1st row (wrong side): 6ch, 1sc into 2nd ch from hook, 1sc into each ch to end, turn.

2nd row: 1ch, 1sc into each sc to end, turn.

3rd row: 1ch, 1sc into each sc to end, 24ch, turn.

4th row: Skip next 24ch, 1sc into each sc to end, turn. Rep 3rd to 4th rows twice more.

9th row: 1ch, 1sc into each sc to end, 8ch, starting from back, wrap 8 ch around the 24ch-loops, sl st into first ch, turn.

Rep 2nd to 9th rows until required length is reached. Fasten off.

Simple Shell Edging

Multiple of 4 sts + 1 st (add 1 st for base chain).

Note: work foundation row if working from a base chain.

Foundation row: 1sc into 2nd ch from hook and each ch to end, turn.

1st row (right side): 1ch, 1sc into first st, or join into an edge, 1ch, 1sc into starting point; counting either sts or equivalent interval, *skip 1 st, 5dc into next st, skip 1 st, 1sc into next st; rep from * to end. Fasten off.

Clematis

Multiple of 20 sts (add 1 st for base chain).

(1 motif for each repeat).

Motif

1st row (petals): *20ch, skip 2 ch, 1sc into each of next 2 ch, 1hdc into next ch, 1dc into each of next 2 ch, 1tr into each of next 2 ch, work 1 tr into each of next 2 ch leaving 1 loop of each on hook, yo and draw through all 3 loops on hook, 1dc into each of next 3 ch, 1hdc into next ch, sl st into each of last 5 ch; rep from * 5 more times. (6 petals)

2nd row (flower base): 1ch, 1sc in base of each of 6 petals, 5ch, turn.

3rd row: Work 1 tr into each of first 5 sc, 2 tr into last sc, leaving 1 loop of each on hook, yo and through all 8 loops on hook, turn.

4th row: 5ch sl st into top of the flower base.

Fasten off.

Header

Using contrasting yarn to that of the motifs,

1st row: Skip 2 ch, 1hdc into each ch to end, turn.

2nd row: 2ch, work 1hdc into each st to end, turn.

Rep 2nd row 3 more times.

Fasten off yarn, join in yarn matching the motifs.

6th row: 2ch, work 1hdc into each st to end, turn.

7th row: 2ch, 1hdc into each of next 9 sts, *yo, insert hook through 5ch-sp on base of motif and through next st, complete st as for a hdc, 1hdc in each of next 20 sts; rep from * to last 10 sts, 1hdc into each st to end.

Join in contrasting yarn.

8th row: 2ch, work 1hdc into each st to end, turn.

Rep 8th row until required depth is reached.

Fasten off.

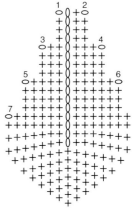

Leaf Fall

(1 motif for each repeat).

Motif

Base chain: 11ch.

1st row (right side): Skip 2 ch (count as 1 sc), 1sc into each ch to last ch, work 3sc into last ch for point, then work back along underside of base chain with 1sc into each ch to end, turn.

2nd row: 1ch (counts as 1 sc), skip 1 st, 1sc into each st up to st at center of point, work 3sc into center st, 1sc into each st to last 3 sts and tch, turn.

3rd to 6th rows: As 2nd row.

Fasten off.

To join the motifs

Arrange the motifs in a line as shown in the photograph, join the contrasting yarn into the outer point, either at tip or base, of the first motif, then, with the working yarn beneath the motif or beneath the motif and the fabric on which it is to appear, and the hook above, sl st along the line of the base chain which forms the center spine of the motif. When the end of the first motif is reached continue in the same way across the next motif.

Continue until required length is reached.

Fasten off.

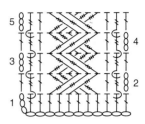

Gwenyth's Cable

Worked lengthways over 12 sts (add 2 sts for base chain).

Special abbreviations: tr/rf (raised triple crochet at the front of the fabric) = yo twice, insert hook from in front and from right to left around the stem of the appropriate stitch, and complete stitch normally; **tr/rb** (raised triple crochet at the back of the fabric) = yo twice, insert hook from behind and from right to left around the stem of the appropriate stitch, and complete stitch normally.

1st row (wrong side): Skip 3 ch (count as 1dc) and 1dc into next ch, work 1dc into each ch to end, turn.

2nd row: 3ch (count as 1dc), skip first st, 1tr/rf around next st, 1dc into next st, skip next 3 sts, 1dtr into each of next 3 sts, going behind last 3dtr work 1dtr into each of

3 sts just skipped, 1dc into next st, 1tr/rf around next st, 1dc tch, turn.

3rd row: 3ch (count as 1dc), skip first st, 1tr/rb around next st, 1dc into next st, skip next 3 sts, 1dtr into each of next 3 sts, going in front of last 3dtr work 1dtr into each of 3 sts just skipped, 1dc into next st, 1tr/rb around next st, 1dc tch, turn.

Rep 2nd and 3rd rows until required length is reached, ending with a 3rd row.

Fold the edging strip in half lengthways and work along the length as folls:

Finishing row: 3ch, *work 2dc round post of last st or tch and tch or first st at beg of same row; rep from * to end. Fasten off.

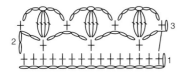

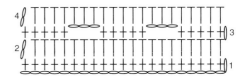

Bobble Dainty

Multiple of 5 sts + 1 st (add 1 st for base chain).

Special abbreviation: 4dc-popcorn = work 4dc into next sc, drop loop from hook, insert hook from front into top of first of these dc, pick up dropped loop and draw through dc, 1ch to secure the popcorn.

1st row (right side): 1sc into 2nd ch from hook, work 1sc into each ch to end, turn.

2nd row: 4ch (count as 1hdc, 2 ch), skip first 2 sc, 1sc into next sc, *5ch, skip 4 sc, 1sc into next sc; rep from * to last 2 sc, 2ch, 1hdc into last sc, turn.

3rd row: 1ch, 1sc into first hdc, 3ch, 1 popcorn into next sc, 3ch, *1sc into next 5ch-arch, 3ch, 1 popcorn into next sc, 3ch; rep from * to last sp, 1sc into 2nd ch of tch.
Fasten off.

Simple Buttonhole

Multiple of 8 sts + 5 sts (add 1 st for base chain).

Suggestion: work a small sample as described and then adjust the spacing, and the multiple, to suit the project.

1st row (right side): 1sc into 2nd ch from hook, work 1sc into each ch, to end, turn.

2nd row: 2ch, 1hdc into each st to end, turn.

3rd row: 1ch, 1sc into each of first 5 sts, *3ch, skip 3 hdc, 1sc into each of next 5 hdc; rep from * to end, turn.

4th row: 2ch, 1hdc into each st or ch to end.
Fasten off.

Clockwork Overlap

(1 motif for each repeat).

First motif

Base ring: 8ch, join with sl st.

1st round: 3ch (count as 1dc), 1dc in ring, *3ch, sl st in top of last dc (picot), 2dc in ring; rep from * until 12th picot is completed, join with sl st in top of 3ch. Fasten off.

Second motif

Base ring: 8ch, join with sl st.

1st round: 3ch, 1dc in ring, 2ch, drop loop from hook, insert hook in any picot of last motif and in dropped loop, draw loop through, 1ch, complete picot on 2nd motif with sl st in first ch, 2dc in ring of 2nd motif, join with picot to next free picot on first motif, continue as in first motif until 12th picot is completed (including the 2 joined picots), join with sl st in top of 3ch. Fasten off.

Rep Second Motif, joining first 2 picots to 7th and 8th picot of previous motif until required length is reached. Position along an edge as shown in the photograph, with the top of alternate motifs on alternate sides of the fabric, and whip stitch to secure.

key

Stitch diagrams are detailed "maps" of fabric showing the right side uppermost. They enable you to see what you are going to do before you start and also where you are at any moment.

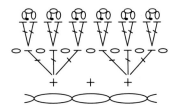

Chart distortions

The stitch symbols are distorted for the sake of clarity. Sometimes, for example, single crochet stitches may look extra long. This is only to show clearly where they go and you should not make artificially long stitches. When the diagram represents a fabric that is not intended to lie flat—for instance, a "gathered" or frilled edging—since the drawing itself has to remain flat, the stitch symbols have to be stretched.

Symbols that accompany stitch symbols

Back/front loop symbols: Stitches that are to be made by inserting the hook under only one of the top two loops are indicated by stitch symbols with heavy and lightweight underlining.

A symbol with a heavyweight underline means insert the hook through the front top loop only to create the next stitch. This is the nearest loop as the row is worked, i.e. front loop on right-side rows but, if the fabric is viewed from the right side, the back loop on wrong-side rows.

A symbol with a lightweight underline means insert the hook through the back top loop only to create the next stitch. This is the furthest loop as the row is worked, i.e. back loop on right-side rows but, if the fabric is viewed from the right side, the front loop on wrong-side rows.

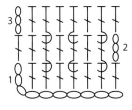

Raised (relief) stitches: When a stitch is to be worked by inserting the hook around the stem of a stitch (instead of under the top two loops), the stitch symbol ends in a "crook" around the appropriate stem.

If the open end is to the left, then a raised stitch will be created on the side being worked and the hook is inserted around the stitch from front to back and to the front again.

If the open end is to the right, then a raised stitch will be created on the reverse of the side being worked and the hook is inserted around the stitch from back to front and to the back again.

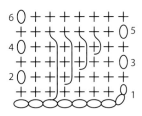

Spikes: The stitch symbol is extended downward to show where the hook is to go through the fabric.

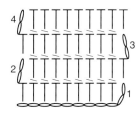

Back bar symbol: On the reverse of half double stitches is a prominent horizontal thread or bar just below the top loops. A tilted lightweight symbol is used to represent this back bar. If stitches are worked into this bar rather than the top loops, both top loops of the stitch appear on the reverse of the side being worked.

Other elements that appear on charts

Arrows: These are used to indicate where stitches should be worked or the passage of a length of crochet.

Figure: Numbers indicate round (or row) numbers.

Foundation rows: These are unlabelled rows that should be worked if an edging is not going to be worked directly along another edge.

Motif style: When the base ring of a motif is drawn as a plain circle, make it by looping the yarn around a finger.

Paler stitches or arrows: These indicate stitches that are worked with the darker stitches or arrows in front.

○
Chain

●
Slip Stitch

+
Single Crochet

T
Half Double Crochet

Ŧ
Double Crochet

Ŧ
Triple Crochet

Ŧ
Double Treble

Ŧ
Triple Treble

Ŧ
Quadruple Treble

Y
Bullion Stitch

●
Bead

Picots = note the pattern method of working the closing slip stitch.

Half double crochet

Double crochet

Triple crochet

Double Treble

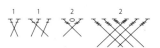
Popcorns: Half double

Popcorns: Double

Crossed Stitches

abbreviations

Most crochet pattern instructions are written out in words. In order to follow these, you must be able to understand the simple jargon, abbreviations and standard conventions.

You are expected to know how to make basic stitches and to be familiar with fabric-making procedures; anything more advanced is spelled out in individual pattern instructions.

Important terms and abbreviations with which you should be familiar include:

A, B, etc = changes of color

alt = alternate

approx = approximate(ly)

beg = begin(ning)

ch sp = chain space

ch(s) = chain(s)

cm = centimeter(s)

cont = continue

dc = double crochet

dec = decrease

dtr = double treble crochet

folls = follows

grp = group

hdc = half double crochet

inc = increase

quin tr = quintuple treble

rem = remaining

rep = repeat

sc = single crochet

sext tr = sextuple treble

sl st = slip stitch

sp = space

st(s) = stitch(es)

tch = turning chain

tog = together

tr = triple crochet

ttr = triple treble crochet

yo = yarn over

Jargon Busting

Base (Foundation) chain = the length of chain made at the beginning of a piece of crochet as a basis for the fabric.

Turning/starting chain = one, or more chains, depending upon the length of stitch required, worked at the beginning of a row (or end of the previous row) as preparation for the new row; sometimes counts as the first stitch in the new row. Called "starting chain" when working "in the round."

Group = several stitches worked into the same place; sometimes called "shell," "fan," etc.

Picot = a run of chain stitches normally brought back on itself and fixed into a decorative loop with a slip stitch or single crochet.

Note: Terms such as "group," "cluster," "picot," and even "shell," "fan," "flower," "petal," "leaf," "bobble," etc, do not denote a fixed arrangement of stitches. Exactly what they mean may be different for each pattern. The procedure is therefore always spelled out at the beginning of each set of pattern instructions and is valid only for that pattern, unless it is stated otherwise.

Yarn over = the stitch-making instruction to wrap the yarn from the ball over the hook (or manipulate the hook around the yarn) in order to make a new loop; always done in an counter-clockwise direction, unless otherwise stated.

Work straight = work over an existing row of stitches without "increasing" (i.e. adding stitches and so making the fabric wider), or "decreasing" (i.e. reducing the number of stitches and so making the fabric narrower). Precise methods of increasing and decreasing vary according to each stitch pattern and circumstances and are detailed in the pattern instructions.

Right/wrong side (RS/WS) = the "right side" is the surface of the fabric intended to be the outside of the finished article and therefore shown in the photographs; the "wrong side" is the inside. If there is a difference, the instructions state which side is facing you as you work the first row and that surface of the fabric is identified and fixed from then on.

Hint: crochet stitches are not the same back and front and so the two sides of a fabric may well be quite different. Even when a stitch pattern has no particular "right side," it is wise to make a positive decision in respect of all separate pieces of the same article, so that the "grain" of the rows can be matched exactly when you join the pieces together.

Front/back = "front" and "back" mean the front and back surfaces of a fabric for the time being as you hold and look at it; these change over every time you turn the work.

Note: In garment pattern instructions the terms "front"and "back" denote the different pieces of the garment.

Multiple = all but the simplest crochet stitch patterns are built around repeated sequences of stitches. In order to make sense of the instructions you must have exactly the right number of stitches in your base row. This number is a multiple of the number of stitches required for one complete sequence—sometimes plus an extra edge stitch or two—and is given at the beginning of each set of instructions.

The number of chains you need for the base chain in order to be able to create the appropriate number of stitches in the base row is also given. For example, "Multiple of 2 sts + 1, (add 1 for base chain)" = make 4, 6, 8, etc chains for a base row of 3, 5, 7, etc stitches; or "Multiple of 8 sts + 3, (add 2 for base chain)" = make 13, 21, 29, etc chains for a base row of 11, 19, 27, etc stitches.

Color note = capital letters A, B, C, D, etc, are used to indicate different yarn colors; when only two colors are involved and one of these is intended to dominate, the terms "main (M)" and "contrast (C)" may be used instead.

Asterisks *, square brackets [ ] and round brackets ( ) = Instructions inside square brackets are to be worked the number of times stated, for example: "[1ch, skip 1ch, 1dc into next st] 5 times."

A sequence of stitches after an asterisk means that the sequence between the asterisk and next semi-colon is to be repeated as stated, for example: "*1ch, skip 1ch, 1dc into next st, 1ch, skip 1ch, 1dc into next 3 sts; rep from * to end."

If no further details are given, as in this case, the end of the sequence will coincide exactly with the end of the row. If there are stitches remaining unworked after the last complete repeat sequence, details of how to complete the row are given, for example: "Rep from * to last 4 sts, ending 1ch, skip 1ch, 1dc into each of last 3 sts, turn." "Rep from * 4 more times" means work that sequence 5 times in all.

Round brackets either enclose additional information—for example: "3ch (count as 1tr), skip first dc."—or group together a sequence of stitches that are to be worked into the same location, for example: "3ch, in next 4ch-sp (1tr, 2ch, 1tr), 3ch."

Charts = Filet crochet patterns, which are based on a regular grid of treble crochet and chain stitches, are much easier to follow from a squared chart when you understand the basic procedures. This type of chart is also used to indicate different colors in Jacquard and Fair Isle patterns, usually based on a plain single crochet fabric.

Stitch diagrams = accurate stitch diagrams show the overall picture at a glance and at the same time indicate precisely every detail of construction. To follow them you need to be familiar with the symbols that represent each stitch.

index

inspiring resources
from Interweave

The Harmony Guides:
Basic Crochet Stitches
Edited by Erika Knight
$22.95
ISBN 978-1-59668-081-4

The Harmony Guides:
Crochet Stitch Motifs
Edited by Erika Knight
$22.95
ISBN 978-1-59668-083-8

The Harmony Guides:
101 Stitches to Crochet
(card deck)
Edited by Erika Knight
$19.95
ISBN 978-1-59668-101-9